KT-173-594

Table of Contents

James Floyd Kelly

Sams **Teach Yourself**

iPad™ 2

in **10 Minutes**

Third Edition

SAMS | 800 East 96th Street, Indianapolis, Indiana 46240

Sams Teach Yourself iPad 2 in 10 Minutes, Third Edition

Copyright © 2012 by Pearson Education, Inc.

ISBN-13: 978-0-672-33585-3

ISBN-10: 0-672-33585-9

Library of Congress Cataloging-in-Publication Data is on file.

Printed in the United States of America

First Printing December 2011

Trademarks

All terms mentioned in this book that are known to be trademarks or service marks have been appropriately capitalized. Sams Publishing cannot attest to the accuracy of this information. Use of a term in this book should not be regarded as affecting the validity of any trademark or service mark.

Warning and Disclaimer

Every effort has been made to make this book as complete and as accurate as possible, but no warranty or fitness is implied. The information provided is on an 'as is' basis. The author and the publisher shall have neither liability nor responsibility to any person or entity with respect to any loss or damages arising from the information contained in this book.

Bulk Sales

Pearson offers excellent discounts on this book when ordered in quantity for bulk purchases or special sales. For more information, please contact

U.S. Corporate and Government Sales
1-800-382-3419
corpsales@pearsontechgroup.com

For sales outside of the U.S., please contact

International Sales
international⌐

Editor in Chief
Greg Wiegand

Acquisitions Editor
Laura Norman

Development Editor
Lora Baughey

Managing Editor
Sandra Schroeder

Project Editor
Mandie Frank

Copy Editor
Charlotte Kughen

Indexer
Lisa Stumpf

Proofreader
Leslie Joseph

Technical Editor
Greg Kettell

Publishing Coordinator
Cindy Teeters

Designer
Gary Adair

Compositor
Mark Shirar

About the Author

James Floyd Kelly is a technology writer from Atlanta, Georgia. James received a Bachelor of Arts degree in English from the University of West Florida and a Bachelor of Science degree in Industrial Engineering from Florida State University.

James has written on numerous technology subjects. He has written books that teach readers how to build CNC machines and 3D printers as well as LEGO robots, and he's written on subjects as diverse as Mint.com (a financial online tool), Open Source software, and the Motorola Xoom tablet.

James' first computer was the original Apple Macintosh (1984), but since then he's mainly been swimming in the waters of Microsoft Windows. But his purchase of the first iPad, followed recently by a purchase of the iPad 2 and then a new Macbook Air, have given him a new outlook on his work life.

James lives with his wife, Ashley, and two sons, and he tries to learn something new every day.

Dedication

For Ryan H. and Jeff D.—thanks, friends, for dragging me kicking and screaming into the world of Apple.

Acknowledgments

I'd like to thank Laura Norman for the chance to (finally) write a book on the iPad. The team at Pearson continues to take my drafts and turn them into better chapters, so a big thanks also goes to the list of names printed a few pages before this one.

I'd also like to thank my tech editor, Greg Kettell, for doing a great job of making sure you're getting accurate instructions on using your iPad 2.

Finally, thanks go to my wife, Ashley, for reasons too numerous to list.

We Want to Hear from You!

As the reader of this book, you are our most important critic and commentator. We value your opinion and want to know what we're doing right, what we could do better, what areas you'd like to see us publish in, and any other words of wisdom you're willing to pass our way.

You can email or write me directly to let me know what you did or didn't like about this book—as well as what we can do to make our books stronger.

Please note that I cannot help you with technical problems related to the topic of this book, and that due to the high volume of mail I receive, I might not be able to reply to every message.

When you write, please be sure to include this book's title and author as well as your name and phone or email address. I will carefully review your comments and share them with the author and editors who worked on the book.

E-mail: consumer@samspublishing.com

Mail: Greg Wiegand
          Editor in Chief
          Sams Publishing
          800 East 96th Street
          Indianapolis, IN 46240 USA

Reader Services

Visit our website and register this book at informit.com/register for convenient access to any updates, downloads, or errata that might be available for this book.

Introduction

The iPad tablet is a huge success. Of course, this statement consists partly of my own opinion, but evidence from sales, customer reviews, and the large number of competitor tablets being released over the last 12+ months all support one clear fact—the iPad has shaken the personal computing world up and there's no going back.

Since the iPad's release in early 2010, the tablet has had a few updates to its operating system, iOS, as well as a completely new version of the tablet called the iPad 2. When the iPad 2 was released it came with version 4.2, and the first edition of this book covered many of the apps and features included with that version of the OS. Now, however, Apple has released a new version, iOS 5, and although it looks and operates just like its predecessor OS, there are some changes—some are easy to spot and others not so easy. And that's where this book comes in.

If you own the first version of the iPad tablet (Let's call it iPad 1 for just a moment) you'll find that most of the features in iOS 5 will work with your device. The iPad 1, however, did not come with a webcam or a digital camera (for taking pictures) so a few of the chapters in this book won't apply to you and you can easily skip over them without missing much (or read them to help you determine whether you wish to upgrade to an iPad 2.)

If you own the iPad 2, however, you'll find that iOS 5 brings a large number of new features (over 200 according to Apple) that are all supported by your version of the tablet.

At the time of this writing, there are no real solid hints of the next version of the iPad tablet and what new features it might possess, but you can be fairly certain that iOS 5 will be the operating system found on the iPad 3 (for lack of a better name) when it is inevitably released.

But for now... we have iOS 5 ready to go for our iPad 1 and iPad 2 devices, so let's jump right in and see what all the noise is about. I think you'll find, as I did, that the new OS is more stable and easier to use as well as possessing some fun new features and tools that will make iPad owners smile.

About This Book

The *Sams Teach Yourself in 10 Minutes* books are all about getting you up to speed fast on the subjects that you need to learn. Each lesson is meant to take about 10 minutes of your time to read so you can immediately apply what you learn before moving on to the next lesson. With this book, my goal is to give you the basic information you need to become proficient in using your iPad.

What you won't necessarily find is complete coverage of every bell and whistle, every hidden feature, and every tucked away option the iPad offers—that would take a book easily two or three times in length, and Que has many titles available such as the *My iPad,* 3rd Edition, that offer much more in-depth coverage. Instead, what you find here is solid coverage of all the pre-installed apps that come with the new iOS 5 and some extra knowledge on pushing your iPad further with apps such as the App Store and the Settings app. You get the basics, but you also get the skills to finish your education confidently knowing how to properly operate your iPad.

Here's a short list of just a few of the things you learn about your iPad and the iOS 5 operating system:

▶ Powering on your iPad and putting it to sleep

▶ Configuring wallpaper and other customizable items

▶ Tweak settings on your iPad to control numerous tasks and controls

▶ Access the Internet via Wi-Fi or 3G Data connectivity

▶ Send and receive email messages

▶ Stay organized with a calendar and reminders

▶ Save and access your contacts and instant message with friends

▶ Install apps from the App Store and update them when necessary

▶ Read books, magazines, and other digital documents

▶ Listen to music, watch videos, and take pictures and video

▶ Access your iCloud account to backup and view your files, photos, and more

▶ View your photos and create slideshows

▶ Discover new uses for your iPad and new accessories

When you finish learning these items and a few more, you can handle anything your iPad throws at you. The iPad is easy to use, and I'd even argue that it's easy to figure out on your own, given enough time. But what's nice about the 10 Minute series is that it reduces the time you need to learn a subject and makes you productive quicker. By the time you reach the end of this book, you'll be proficient with your iPad and have the skills to dive deeper with it without concerns of messing things up.

Who This Book Is For

If you can already navigate your iPad with the greatest of ease, moving apps from page to page, downloading and tweaking apps from the App store like a professional programmer, and moving photos, sending emails, and browsing the web, you're not likely to find this book of much use.

If, however, you are new to the iPad and want to have some basic skills before you head off on your own, this book can help. If you are the kind of person who needs some basic instructions on the latest iOS version without a lot of techno-babble, you'll also find this book useful. Whether you just opened the box of your new iPad or have just updated your existing iPad from version 4 to version 5, with the instructions in this book, you'll spend less time reading and more time using your iPad.

What Do I Need to Use This Book?

For not-so-obvious reasons right now, the iPad 2 is the best choice of tablet as you read through this book—it has the camera and webcam that the iPad 1 lacks, and you find lessons on using both of those features. But iPad 1 users should know that 90% of this book is just as relevant to an iPad 1 running iOS 5.

The book does not cover upgrading your iPad 1 or iPad 2 to iOS 5. This is not difficult to do, but it is beyond the scope of this book. Just know that the upgrade is handled using iTunes and you have the choice whether to update or not. Hopefully by the time you finish this book, you have some good reasons to agree to the update.

If you need more details about the upgrade from iOS 4 to iOS 5 before you make the jump, you should do a quick Google search for "Instructions for upgrading iPad to iOS 5" to find a good selection of tutorials that show you how the upgrade works. You can also check the Apple.com website for information on what features iOS 5 offers; a good place to start is http://www.apple.com/ios/ios5/. Expect to spend 10 to 20 minutes reading all about the latest and greatest features iOS 5 brings.

Conventions Used in This Book

In addition to the text and figures in this book, you also encounter some special boxes labeled Tip, Note, or Caution.

TIP: Tips offer helpful shortcuts or easier ways to do something.

NOTE: Notes are extra bits of information related to the text that might help you expand your knowledge or understanding.

CAUTION: Cautions are warnings or other important information you need to know about consequences of using a feature or executing a task.

Possible Updates to iOS 5

The instructions and figures found in this book were taken with the beta version (test version) of iOS 5—I began using the operating system long before its release so that this book could be ready and available for you when the actual operating system was released.

Because I used the beta version, there is a slight chance that some of the steps or figures might not match up exactly to those experienced with the final release version of iOS 5. Rest assured, any changes made by Apple are likely to be minor and shouldn't affect how you learn the new operating system. When in doubt, always consult the iPad User Guide covered in Lesson 3 or point your web browser at Apple.com or Google.com to get a quick answer.

LESSON 1

Your iPad 2 Overview

In this lesson, you learn about the buttons, cameras, speaker, and other options that make up the iPad's exterior. You also learn how to turn the iPad on and off, put it to sleep, perform the various gestures used in conjunction with the tablet's touchscreen to open apps, play games, and more.

The iPad's Exterior

You're probably anxious to start using your iPad, but you'll be much better prepared if you spend a few brief moments learning about the iPad's features such as its various buttons, the touchscreen, and the other options found on its exterior.

The first thing you notice about the iPad is its lack of a keyboard. The iPad is called a tablet, which implies it's meant to be carried and held as you use it. (This doesn't mean you can't set the iPad on a table or prop it up on a stand, but the iPad's strength is its portability, enabling you to use it while you sit, stand, walk, or, crazy as it sounds, run.)

The iPad has an assortment of buttons and other features on its external shell. Let's take a tour of the iPad's outside before we turn our attention to its software "insides."

The Touchscreen

Most everything you do with the iPad is done via the touchscreen. As a replacement for a mouse and keyboard, the touchscreen enables you to tap on applications you want to open and run, type using the on-screen keyboard, and use your fingers to drag, twist, and perform other gestures (read more on gestures later in the chapter).

The touchscreen is made with a special type of glass that resists finger-prints and is extremely durable. You shouldn't drop heavy items on the screen (any items, actually), but it might surprise you how well it avoids scratches. Fingerprints, smudges, and water droplets are all easily wiped away with a clean cloth.

Figure 1.1 shows the iPad's touchscreen and the on-screen keyboard you use to type email messages, notes, and more.

FIGURE 1.1   The on-screen keyboard replaces an external keyboard.

Notice in Figure 1.1 that the on-screen keyboard takes up about half the screen space. This is because the iPad in this example is held so that it is wider than it is taller, which is called the Horizontal View (also called Landscape). You can shrink the keyboard a bit by rotating the iPad 90 degrees as shown in Figure 1.2. Doing so rotates whatever is shown on the screen and displays it in Vertical View, also known as Portrait or Book View, because you hold the iPad so that it's taller than it is the way most books are.

If you don't like the way the iPad's touchscreen auto-rotates when you turn the tablet, there is a way to disable the auto rotation. I show you how to do this later in the chapter.

FIGURE 1.2   Rotate the iPad and the screen view changes.

NOTE: **Some Apps Work in Only One Viewing Mode**

Some of the apps you use with your iPad are created to work in only one viewing mode—Horizontal or Vertical. If you have the Rotate Lock enabled and you open an app while holding the iPad in Vertical Mode and the text or images on the screen appear sideways, you need to rotate the tablet to view it in Horizontal View. The same goes for holding the iPad in Horizontal View—you might have to rotate it to Vertical View to properly view an app that is designed for vertical viewing.

The Power/Sleep Button

If you look carefully at Figure 1.2, you notice that the iPad is held in Vertical View such that the small round button is at the bottom of the tablet and the small black dot is at the top. (That black dot is actually the iPad's webcam.) What's great about the iPad is that you can flip the device 180 degrees so that the black dot/webcam is at the bottom and the small button (called the Home button) is at the top. This typically won't affect what you view on the screen; but throughout the remainder of this book, let's assume that when the iPad is in Vertical Mode, the Home button is at the bottom and the webcam is at the top.

When you hold the iPad in Vertical Mode, notice that in the top-right corner you see a small black button like the one shown in Figure 1.3. This is the Power/Sleep button.

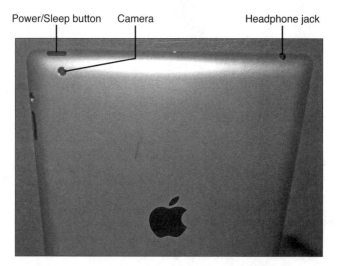

FIGURE 1.3　The Power/Sleep button on the top-right edge.

Your iPad has three operating modes: Powered Off, Powered On, and Sleep.

If you've never turned on your iPad, you need to press and hold the Power button for about five seconds. The Apple icon appears briefly as the iPad boots up (turns on). Follow the on-screen instructions to provide your iPad with some basic information (such as the language you want to use).

After the iPad is on, you can turn it off completely (saving battery power) by pressing and holding the Power button again for five seconds. Hold it down until a small red slider button appears with the Slide to Power Off message. If you want to completely turn off your iPad, press the red button and slide your finger to the right. This tells your iPad to completely power down.

The iPad has an outstanding battery life, so the other option available to you is to simply put the iPad to sleep. When the iPad is powered up, press the Power/Sleep button quickly (three seconds or less) and the touchscreen turns off. Your iPad still draws a bit of power in this mode. Another fast tap on the Power/Sleep button turns the iPad back on.

Figure 1.4 shows the screen that displays when the iPad comes out of Sleep mode. You need to tap and slide the Slide to Unlock button at the bottom of the screen. Slide it to the right and your iPad is ready to use again.

FIGURE 1.4   Bring your iPad out of Sleep mode with a finger swipe.

NOTE: **Sleep versus Powered Off**
When powered off, your iPad is not using battery power. If you need to conserve battery power and do not have access to your iPad's charger, powering down your iPad can often mean the difference between a dead iPad and a few extra minutes (or hours) of service. Sleep, however, really doesn't consume that much battery power, and the tablet powers on much faster from Sleep Mode. You quickly discover which mode works best for your situation.

Headphones and Speaker

Your iPad has two methods for producing sound. The first is the single headphone jack found on the top-left edge of the tablet. You need to use headphones with a 3.5mm headphone jack.

Flip your iPad over to find the tablet's speaker near the bottom left edge. The iPad's speaker can produce sounds at a decent volume, but it does have its limits. You may find that in noisy environments (such as your favorite coffee shop), the speaker just isn't capable of a sufficient volume for you to hear. You may want to carry a small pair of headphones for times when you want to listen to your music privately or need to hear what's being said in a video or webchat.

Volume and Mute/Rotate Lock

Whether you listen to headphones or use the iPad's speaker, you can increase or decrease the sound using the volume controls on the right side of the iPad. Just above the volume control button is another button that can mute or unmute sound. Figure 1.5 shows the Mute and Volume Control buttons.

You can reconfigure the Mute button to serve as a Rotate Lock button. Earlier, I mentioned that rotating your iPad causes it to automatically rotate whatever is displayed on the screen. You can disable this auto-rotation using the Rotate Lock button.

By default, this button is configured as a Mute/Unmute button when you first turn on your iPad. To reconfigure this button to serve as the Rotate Lock button, you need to access the iPad's Settings, which you can read about in Lesson 2, "Your iPad's Settings."

Webcam

Mute button

Volume control

Home button

FIGURE 1.5 Control the volume or mute the sound altogether. (Side view photo credit: Jason R. Rich.)

Camera and Webcam

When holding your iPad in Vertical View, the iPad's webcam is located near the top of the tablet, just above the top-edge of the touchscreen. In Lesson 9 you learn how to use the webcam, but for now all you need to know about it is that it operates in both Horizontal View and Vertical View. Rotating the iPad is not a problem for the webcam.

While holding your iPad in Vertical View, quickly flip it around and you see the iPad's built-in digital camera in the upper-left corner. You learn more about the iPad's camera and how it is used in Lesson 9.

NOTE: **The iPad's Camera Quality Isn't All That Great**
The quality of the images provided by the iPad 2's digital camera is a sore spot for many iPad 2 users. Most mobile phones these days have better cameras and take higher quality photos, but in a pinch you can use the iPad 2 to snap some decent photos, but they're unlikely to be suitable for framing.

Charging Port

On the bottom edge of the iPad is a wide port used to charge your tablet. This port has additional uses (such as transferring photos from a digital camera with a special cable), but you use it most often to simply recharge the iPad's battery.

> CAUTION: **Be Careful with the Charging Port**
> The charger that comes with your iPad is a fragile little thing—when inserting the cable into the charging port, take care to insert it directly into the port; make sure it's not at an angle. When removing the cable, pinch on the cable's end and pull it gently out of the charging port to prevent damage to the sensitive parts tucked into the charging port as well as the plug at the end of the cable.

When you insert the cable into the charging port, you hear a slight beep from the iPad that lets you know it's getting power and that charging has begun.

The Home Button

If you hold the iPad in Vertical View, the Home button is at the bottom of the tablet, just beneath the touchscreen's lower edge. This little button has other functions that you learn about as you read through the other lessons, but the function for which you use the button most is returning to the Home screen.

Here's the key to the Home button: pressing it at any time, whether you're playing a game or typing up an email or browsing the Web, immediately takes you to the iPad's Home screen. But which one?

That's right—you can have multiple Home screens. But only one of them is the primary Home screen. Confused yet? Don't be. This becomes easier to understand with a quick overview of how you use the iPad, also referred to as *interfacing with your device*, but I promise to keep my terms as non-techy as possible.

The Dock and Home Screen

With your iPad turned on for the first time, you see a screen like the one in Figure 1.6. This is the Home screen.

FIGURE 1.6   The iPad's Home screen.

Along the bottom edge of the screen, whether you view it horizontally or vertically (Figure 1.6 is a Vertical View image), you see the Dock. Above the Dock are small icons that each represent an app (short for application) and stay on the screen at all times.

Let's look at the Dock first. In Figure 1.6, you notice four apps in the Dock: Safari, Mail, Photos, and Music. Up to six apps can be placed on the Dock, so I have room to add two more.

Above the dock in Figure 1.6 are the sixteen apps that come standard with the iPad. (It's possible this number might change if Apple adds or removes apps, so don't stress if you have 15 or 17 or some other number of apps.) Up to 20 apps can be displayed on the Home screen. In Vertical View that presents as five rows and four columns and in Horizontal View it changes to four rows and five columns.

You have to look carefully, but on the Home screen are two additional items. Sandwiched between the apps and the Dock are a small magnifying glass and one or more dots. If you only see one dot, then you only have one Home screen. Additional home screens (which you learn about later in this lesson) are each represented by a dot.

NOTE: **The Primary or Original Home Screen**

If you see multiple dots then the left-most white dot (next to the magnifying glass) corresponds to the original Home screen. I sometimes refer to this as the primary Home screen. I use the terms *original* and *primary* to remind you that later on you'll likely have multiple screens with apps on them, but you only ever have one Home screen that a single press of the Home button returns you to—and that will be the *primary* or *original* Home screen.

Swiping to the right will call up the Search screen shown in Figure 1.7.

The Search Screen

There are, three methods for accessing the Search screen. I find option 1 to be the fastest for me, but use what works best for you:

  1. If you are on any other Home screen besides the primary Home screen, touch and hold your finger anywhere on the touchscreen, with the exception of the Dock, and drag your finger to the right. (This is called a swipe, and I talk about it and other gestures shortly.) Repeat this gesture until you reach the Search page shown in Figure 1.7. Notice that as you swipe to the right, the white dot moves closer to the magnifying glass, one dot for each non-primary Home screen that you bypass.

2. If you are on the primary Home screen tap the Home button once.

3. If you are not on the primary Home screen tap the Home button once (taking you to the primary Home screen), and then tap the Home button again and the Search screen appears. There must be a slight pause between Home button taps or this shortcut won't work.

No matter how you get to the Search screen, when there you can type in a keyword or keywords using the on-screen keyboard. As you type keywords, a list appears as shown in Figure 1.8.

FIGURE 1.7 The Search page is there when you need it.

FIGURE 1.8   Search results are a finger tap away.

Search results are organized using an icon that represents the app needed
to access what you are searching for. In Figure 1.8 you see a search for all
instances of the term HOA (Home Owners Association). You can see that
there are a couple of Calendar items (indicated by the Calendar icon) and
three email items (indicated by the Email icon). The Search screen also
provides you with the option to search the Web or Wikipedia. You then tap
any of the search results to immediately go to that item.

Tap the Home button to be returned to the primary Home screen. It's now
time to practice navigating the iPad's touchscreen.

Gestures

Gestures are such a key component to using the iPad. Without an external
keyboard, the iPad uses the touchscreen as its primary method of control.

From typing text using the on-screen keyboard to turning features on and off with a tap of your finger, the iPad is all about using your hand and anywhere from one to five fingers to perform tasks.

But these tasks aren't done by simply tapping one, two, or even five fingers on the screen—they require a specific movement of your fingers while in contact with the screen. This is called a gesture, and just like a wave hello or a two finger salute, you want to learn the various gestures that are supported by your iPad to create a more fun and productive experience.

Swiping

If you've followed along up to this point, you're already a pro at swiping and dragging because you've moved between Home screen(s) and the Search screen and you've powered down and awoken your iPad from Sleep mode.

Swiping is a fast flick of a finger to the left or right, similar to flipping a page in a book or magazine. With your iPad, you use the Swipe gesture a lot. It's like rubbing an eyelash off the screen; you quickly place, swish, and lift your finger, all in less than a second.

Dragging is similar to a Swipe, but instead of lifting your finger quickly, you hold it to the touchscreen until whatever action you need to accomplish is complete. Think of tracing the outline of a circle or square on a piece of paper; you hold your finger down but move it along the shape's outline. Trust me—you'll be a pro at dragging in no time, too.

So what other types of gestures does the iPad recognize? Well, there are quite a few of them, and each of them is useful for certain apps, as I explain in the following sections.

Pinching

The Pinch gesture is an easy one to do—touch your thumb and pointer finger anywhere on the touchscreen and then move them together to mimic a soft pinch. You don't have to squeeze them tightly like you would if you were pinching something hard—just bring them together quickly and release.

As you learn to use your iPad's various apps, you likely discover that there are many uses for the Pinch gesture. Some apps (especially games) use the Pinch gesture to perform their own special actions, but the one action you see where the Pinch gesture is used most often is shrinking an image (such as a photo) or a page of text. (There are other ways that this shrinking action is helpful, and I cover them more specifically in later lessons.)

Take a look at Figure 1.9. What you see here is the Que blog that I'm reading at the moment on my iPad. Notice how the text on the right side of the screen is cut off?

FIGURE 1.9   One of the two columns of text is not completely visible.

If I place my thumb and pointer finger on the screen and slowly move them together, the image on the screen shrinks. I don't have to complete the pinch gesture (by bringing thumb and pointer all the way together to touch), and I can stop the gesture at any time when I'm happy with the resizing of the on-screen text or image. Figure 1.10 shows the same web page, but this time both columns of text are readable.

FIGURE 1.10   The website is resized and both columns are readable.

Great—I've resized the screen with a pinch gesture so I can read both vertical columns of articles. But notice that the two articles at the bottom of the screen also now have unreadable text that continues below the screen's edge. What do I do?

Simple—I can now use a Swipe or Drag gesture. Instead of swiping or dragging left or right, I want to swipe or drag up toward the top of the touchscreen. A quick swipe gesture causes the webpage to scroll fast, and I might miss something important as the page flies up. A drag gesture is probably the best solution as I can leave my finger on the screen and move it up and down as I read the screen. Figure 1.11 shows that I scrolled the webpage up using a drag gesture so that I can view the next few articles.

FIGURE 1.11   Pinch and drag gestures are great for web browsing.

Additional swipe or drag gestures are obviously needed as I can see more articles are extending past the bottom of the screen.

The pinch gesture and its companion, the reverse pinch, are extremely useful as you navigate your iPad. Websites, photos, maps, and more are all services and features that are necessary to shrink in order to view properly.

Reverse Pinching

It's probably obvious how a reverse pinch (also called an unpinch) is performed and what it does, but let's go over it anyway. If a pinch gesture pulls the thumb and pointer finger together and shrinks an image or a page of text then a reverse pinch does the opposite. To enlarge a photo on the screen, or maybe zoom in on a map so you can view street names, you place a touching thumb and pointer finger on the screen and then move them apart.

As with the Pinch gesture, you can control the speed and the amount of text or image enlargement by executing the reverse pinch slowly and pulling your fingers off the screen when you've achieved a suitable level of zoom.

Figure 1.12 shows the same webpage shown in Figure 1.11, but in this case I zoom in the maximum amount possible and only a fraction of the "Introducing Spotify" article is visible.

FIGURE 1.12   Maximum zoom—minimum information.

Zooming in on photos and text isn't just for those with aging vision. The Pinch and Reverse Pinch gestures enable you to resize photos, text, and any other content displayed on the touchscreen to suit your need.

Not all content is resizable, however. In many of the apps you use, the text or imagery cannot be enlarged or shrunk, so the two gestures won't always work.

Using the Multi-Finger Gesture

This isn't a reference to anything obscene here. The latest version of the iPad's operating system supports a number of extra gestures that require the use of four or five fingers. That may sound funny, but these gestures are useful.

Four-Finger Pinch

First, if you have an open app on the screen, you can immediately return to the Home screen by touching four (or five fingers—either number works) to the touchscreen and pulling them together. It's like a Pinch gesture, but all your fingers must come together to a point for this feature to work. Do it correctly and it performs the same action as pressing the Home button.

Four-Finger Slide

You learn about the pros and cons of multi-tasking in Lesson 13, but for now all you need to know is that the iPad is capable of fast-switching between apps that you have open, effectively sharing the iPad's processing power by having multiple apps running at the same time. In order to view all the apps you have running at once (and to jump to another one with a simple tap of your finger), place four (or five fingers) side-by-side on to the touchscreen and push up an inch or two. You should see something similar to the Dock at the bottom of the screen (but it's not the Dock). Figure 1.13 shows the multitasking bar that appears—there are currently six apps running in the background and you can touch any one of them to immediately open and jump to that app. Only six apps can be displayed at a time on the bar, so use a Swipe gesture (to the left) to scroll through additional apps that are open.

FIGURE 1.13   The Multitasking bar allows for fast jumps between apps.

> NOTE: **Multitasking Bar—No Gestures Required**
>
> Just to be thorough, the other method for accessing the multitask-
> ing bar is to simply tap the Home button twice in quick succession.
> Tap too slow and you just remain on the Home screen, but two
> quick taps should pull up the multitasking bar.

Four-Finger Swipe

The final multi-finger gesture I want to introduce enables you to move
between apps that are currently open. You just learned how to view the
multitasking bar, so if you've got two or more apps open at the same time,

you can place four (or five fingers) together on the touchscreen and drag them left or right (up is used to view the multitasking bar, down to hide it).

Hands down, this is my favorite multi-finger gesture and I use it constantly. The ability to move between apps without the need to return to the Home screen and tap an app to open it? Priceless.

Additional Home Screens

Before we wrap up this chapter, let's look at how to create multiple Home screens. As you read on, remember that only one of the Home screens is the primary Home screen that is opened whenever you press the Home button.

You learn in Lesson 7, "Using the App Store," how to download apps from the App Store—either free or as a purchase. If you download a new app to your iPad and the primary Home screen has 20 apps already displayed, the new app is automatically added after you create a new Home screen.

Figure 1.14 shows a new Home screen. How do you know it's not the primary Home screen? Look again at the dots indicated in Figure 1.14 and you see that the left-most dot is no longer white. There are two dots now, so you know you're not viewing the primary Home screen because the dot furthest from the magnifying glass is now white.

What if you want to drag one of the apps from the primary Home screen to this new Home screen?—Follow these easy steps:

1. Press the Home button or swipe to the right to return to the primary Home screen.

2. Press on the app you want to move (or any app, really) and hold until the apps start wiggling.

3. When all the apps are wiggling, touch and hold your finger on the app you want to move and then drag it to the right until it's almost going off the edge of the screen. When you drag it far enough to the right (or left, if you're moving an app from another Home screen to one closer to the primary Home screen), the screen turns like a page and enables you to place the dancing app

where you want it. Lift your finger and press the Home button again to stop the wiggling and lock in the app's new location. If you move the app off of the right-most Home screen (indicated by the right-most white dot) a new Home screen is automatically created.

Figure 1.14 shows that the Settings app is moved to the newly created Home screen. In addition, some additional apps are downloaded and placed on the screen.

FIGURE 1.14   Moving apps from screen to screen.

You might have noticed two things in Figure 1.14. First, a few of the apps have a circle in their upper-left corners with an X in the center. Tap this X to delete the app from your iPad. Don't worry—if you tap one by accident a pop-up window displays that lets you confirm the deletion or cancel this action. This delete button only appears when the apps are wiggling (after pressing and holding an app for one or more seconds). If an app does not have the delete button on it then it is one of the default apps provided by Apple; you cannot remove these apps.

The second thing you might have noticed is the icon that looks like an app (and is named Education) but that also has five small icons inside it. This is the iPad's version of a folder. You can use folders to group apps (such as all your game apps in a Games folder), but you can also use them to reduce the number of apps on a screen and free up space.

I personally don't like using too many Home screens. Instead, as the number of apps increases on my iPad, I create folders such as Games, Education, Productivity, and so on, and I collect my apps inside these folders.

A single tap on a folder app opens it. It ends up looking almost like a Home screen page itself. When a folder is open, a single tap on an app opens and runs the app as usual.

Summary

In this lesson you learned all about the iPad's exterior and the various components it offers such as the Home button, speakers, and webcam. You also learned how to use gestures to navigate around on the touchscreen, view the multitasking bar, create new Home screens, and move or delete apps.

LESSON 2

Your iPad's Settings

In this lesson, you learn about configuring your iPad using the Settings app. You can easily and quickly do everything from joining a Wi-Fi network to changing your wallpaper to configuring a security code using this single app.

The Settings App

You're probably ready to start using your iPad, but I think you'll find using the iPad much more enjoyable if you learn to tweak some of the settings that make the iPad "your own." This means changing a few things such as the wallpaper image, notification sounds, and the screen brightness.

There are way too many settings to cover in one lesson, but in this lesson I do my best to introduce you to the ones that will likely have the biggest effect as you learn more about the features of your iPad. I haven't covered the Safari app yet—used to browse the web—but be aware that the iPad's User Guide is in there, and you can reference it for any additional information you need regarding the Settings app...and everything else, really. If you want to access the User Guide, jump to Lesson 3 to learn about how to access it and then come back here...I'll wait.

Keep in mind that it's very difficult to do something wrong on your iPad. Most settings that you tweak can be undone, and it's very rare to make a setting selection that deletes or removes something without a warning.

Don't let the Settings app scare you—the more comfortable you are with making changes in the Settings app, the more useful your iPad becomes.

Let's start by opening up the Settings app using the icon shown in Figure 2.1.

FIGURE 2.1   The Settings app on your iPad.

The Settings app should be on the primary Home screen, but it's possible you've dragged it to a new Home screen (refer to Lesson 1, "Your iPad 2 Overview," for how to do this). Locate the Settings app and tap it once to open it. When the Settings app opens, you see a screen similar to the one shown in Figure 2.2. There might be some subtle differences, especially if you've already installed additional apps from the App Store (see Lesson 7, "Using the App Store"), but these differences won't interfere with the remaining discussions in this lesson.

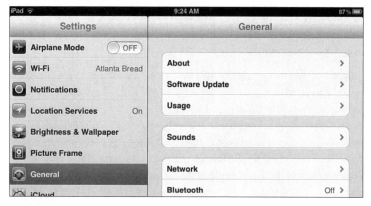

FIGURE 2.2   The Settings screen is open and ready.

Whether you view the Settings screen in Horizontal View or Vertical View, a list of settings that can be changed displays down the left side of the screen.

Throughout this lesson, I refer to the left side of the screen as the Settings List and the right side of the screen as the Setting Options.

Airplane Mode

The first item you see in the Settings List is Airplane Mode. By default, it is set to Off, but you or someone else might have turned it on.

Airplane Mode disables all types of wireless communication that your iPad has installed—this includes Wi-Fi, 3G Data, and Bluetooth. It's called Airplane Mode because when you get on an airplane you're typically asked to disable all communication devices at different times—before takeoff, just after takeoff, and prior to landing.

This is a simple toggle button that helps ensure that the device is in compliance. Although there is much debate as to whether wireless communication signals actually interfere with an airplane's electronics, it's still a rule whether you believe it or not, so touch your finger to the on-screen toggle switch and you see it switch to On as shown in Figure 2.3.

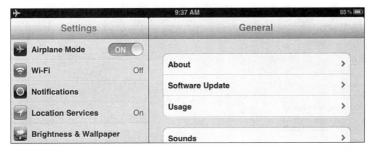

FIGURE 2.3   Airplane Mode is turned On.

Tap your finger again on the Airplane Mode toggle switch and you see it switch to the Off position. Easy enough. You've just learned how to make your first iPad settings change. (While in the air, you can re-enable Wi-Fi during the flight if your plane supports the service but 3G support will continue to be disabled.)

Wi-Fi

All versions of the iPad support Wi-Fi, so the next item you see in the Settings List is Wi-Fi. If the Wi-Fi is turned off as shown in Figure 2.4, tap the toggle button on the right side of the screen to turn it on.

Toggle Button

FIGURE 2.4   Wi-Fi may be turned off on your iPad.

After turning on Wi-Fi, your iPad attempts to locate one or more wireless networks within range. Notice in Figure 2.5 that my iPad has already detected and joined the Atlanta Bread network. This is indicated by the check mark next to the name of the network.

Joined Network

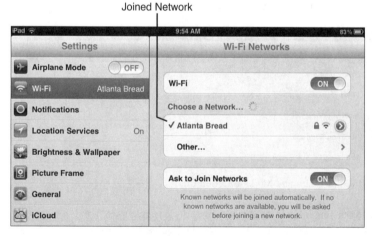

FIGURE 2.5   Your iPad may join a known network automatically.

If your iPad doesn't automatically join an existing network but you see one or more network names in the list, you can attempt to join one if you have the correct password for that network. You know a password is required if there is a small padlock icon to the right of the name as shown in Figure 2.6.

Password Required

FIGURE 2.6 A padlock icon means a network requires a password.

If you see a network listed without a padlock icon, that network is open. An open network could be a free-to-use network such as those found in some airports or restaurants, or it could mean you've discovered a private network that is not properly protected.

> TIP: **Open Networks Aren't Always Safe**
>
> Wi-Fi networks that are open and don't require a password are not necessarily safe to use. Be wary of joining networks that don't require passwords as they can be used to spy on your activity and collect information (such as personal data) from your iPad. As a rule, I only join networks that I know and recognize as legitimate— my coffee shop, my own home network (password protected), and a few businesses with waiting rooms, such as my mechanic and my dentist office.

To join a network (that requires a password), tap once on the network's name or the padlock icon. You see a screen appear like the one in Figure 2.7. Enter the password; the actual password will be obscured with dots.

Tap the Join button on the screen (see Figure 2.7) or on the on-screen keyboard and, if the password is entered correctly, you see the check mark appear next to the network name (refer to Figure 2.5).

FIGURE 2.7   Enter a password to join a Wi-Fi network.

If you do not see a network appear in the list, you can click the Other button to provide the Name of the network and the type of Security (WEP, WPA, WPA2, and more) required. This information needs to be provided to you, along with the password, by the person or organization offering the Wi-Fi service.

NOTE: **Not All Wi-Fi Networks Are Visible**

You might be wondering why a network that you can join doesn't show up in the list. When a company or individual configures a Wi-Fi network, there is often an option to hide the network name, also called the SSID, or Service Set Identifier. If a network name is hidden, you can still join it but you must enter in the name, its type of security (basically, how passwords and data are encrypted to prevent bad guys from reading it), and the password to join a hidden network.

After you join a Wi-Fi network, your iPad is configured to allow you to browse the web, send and receive email, download files, and much more—basically the same things you do with an internet connection on a computer or laptop. I discuss email and web browsing later in the book, but for now you can be happy knowing that you know how to properly configure your iPad to join a Wi-Fi network.

Notifications

Your iPad is capable of alerting you when you receive new email as well as popping up a reminder about that doctor's appointment later today. But it's not just email and calendar notifications that can be turned on and off; your iPad's apps are also capable of getting your attention. Best of all, you can choose how these notifications are presented to you and whether or not they interfere with your current iPad activity (such as playing a game or chatting with a friend with the webcam).

The third item in the Settings List is the Notifications option, and you can see in Figure 2.8 that it has quite a few configurable items on the right side of the screen.

I don't have space to go over every app and every tweak that the Notifications offer to you, so I encourage you to experiment and tap on those apps that I don't show you here. You really can't do anything that cannot be undone, so feel free to play around with the Notifications options and see what works best for you.

The first thing you need to know is that the Notification Center is hidden from view on your iPad. Touch and hold a finger to the time at the very top of the screen and drag your finger down; you see a box drop down like the one in Figure 2.9.

FIGURE 2.8   Notifications help you to stay organized and aware.

FIGURE 2.9   The Notification Center is hidden from view.

I currently have no notifications, but that's about to change. First, I'd like to see unread emails that have arrived without opening the Mail app (covered in Lesson 4). I tap the Mail icon (refer to Figure 2.8) which opens a screen like the one shown in Figure 2.10.

FIGURE 2.10   Configuring the Mail app for the Notification Center.

First, I need to turn on the ability for the Mail app to send notifications to the Notification Center by tapping the toggle button (refer to Figure 2.10) at the top of the list of options.

NOTE: **Pop-Ups Can Be Useful**

I tend to enter appointments in my Calendar with a 1 or 2 hour reminder set. I like to configure the Calendar app in the Notifications settings using the Alerts option so that a pop-up alert appears on the screen, forcing me to acknowledge it. If I configured those reminders to appear in the Notifications Center that is only visible when I pull it down, I might miss an appointment. Keep this in mind for other apps where you might prefer a pop-up alert instead of a hidden alert.

Next, the Alert Style is currently set to None (again, refer to Figure 2.10). I can choose to have a list of unread emails appear in the Notification Center that is hidden from view or I can choose to have an alert pop up on the screen every time a message arrives. That last option becomes annoying fast, so I choose the Banners option (as opposed to the Alerts option) as seen in Figure 2.11.

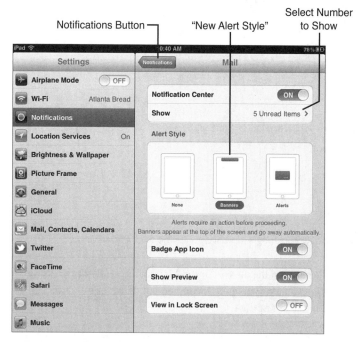

FIGURE 2.11   Configure Mail to show unread messages.

Other options on the Mail app's configuration screen include the ability to increase the number of unread emails that appear (currently set to 5 but changeable to 1, 5, 10, or 20). This is changed by tapping the Show option shown in Figure 2.11.

Finally, your Mail app icon (located by default in the Dock) is capable of displaying a small number in its upper-right corner that indicates the number of unread email messages. This is called a Badge, and you can turn this feature On and Off using the Badge App Icon setting shown in

Figure 2.11. I have it set to On, along with the Show Preview, which displays the first few lines of text of any unread messages in the Notification Center. Turn these On or Off based on your own preferences.

When you finish configuring an app's Notification settings, tap the Notifications button (refer to Figure 2.11) and you are returned to the list of other apps that can be configured for Notifications. You need to open each one and examine the different settings that you can apply. Each app is unique in terms of its notification settings, so set aside some time to open them all up and see what notification options are available.

Location Services

Your iPad is capable of determining its location (and hopefully your location if the iPad is in your possession) using Location Services. Without getting too technical, your iPad can use information received via the GPS, 3G, and Wi-Fi services you join to figure out its/your location. This information can be used to provide location information for photographs you take, for example. It can also be used to help locate your iPad if it's ever stolen or lost.

The Location Services settings can get quite complicated, and there are many reasons you might or might not want to use it—discussions that go beyond the scope of this introductory book. If you want additional details about the pros and cons of Location Services as well as instructions on how to better use it, read the following article from Apple:

http://support.apple.com/kb/HT4084

It's important to note that the Find My iPad service (which helps you locate a stolen or lost iPad) does not work if Location Services is disabled. If you choose to disable Location Services, tap the toggle button shown in Figure 2.12 and then tap the Turn Off button on the Alert that appears.

NOTE: **Disable the Camera App's Ability to Embed Location Data**
I recommend that you disable Location Services for the iPad's Camera app. If it's already set to Off as shown in Figure 2.12, leave it that way so that your address cannot possibly be obtained

from any digital photos you take and share over the internet. Digital photos can have information embedded in the file such as the file size, type of camera used, and more...including the possible location of that great photo of your new car sitting in the driveway. Don't give bad guys information on how to find you and your possessions.

FIGURE 2.12   Location Services can be disabled.

Location Services is covered in much more detail in *My iPad* from Que.

Brightness & Wallpaper

The Brightness & Wallpaper settings are so easy to overlook, but I encourage you to check them out. The brightness of the iPad's screen has an effect on battery life, so it's worth spending a few moments to try to find the lowest lighting level on your iPad that you can tolerate while still enjoying using your tablet.

Tap the Brightness & Wallpaper option in the Settings List and you see a short list of configurable items on the right side of the screen as shown in Figure 2.13.

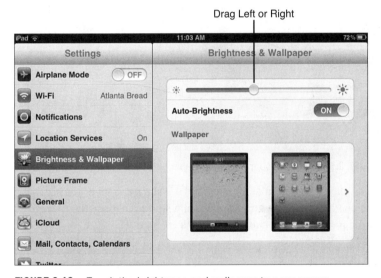

FIGURE 2.13   Tweak the brightness and wallpaper to save power.

You can choose to allow the iPad to set the screen's brightness by leaving the Auto-Brightness toggle button set to On. I prefer to have some control, so I turn it Off and drag the small circle indicated in Figure 2.13 to the left or right. Dragging it to the right brightens the screen; dragging it left darkens the screen.

Some apps have their own built-in brightness controls (many eBook readers enable you to change the brightness without leaving the app and opening the Settings app), but not all. Adjust it according to your needs, or simply let your iPad adjust it automatically by leaving the Auto-Brightness button set to On.

Below the Auto-Brightness setting is the Wallpaper control. Tap the small chevron (the right-pointing arrow) and you are presented with two options—Wallpaper or Camera Roll—as shown in Figure 2.14.

FIGURE 2.14   Choose your iPad's wallpaper.

If you click the chevron to the right of the Wallpaper option, you see a selection of 30 or more images provided with the iOS operating system. Tap an image to select it as the wallpaper for your iPad.

If you click the chevron to the right of Camera Roll, you can choose from images stored in the Photos app (more on this in Lesson 11), include digital photos you've taken with the iPad's built-in camera.

I've not read any studies that show how battery life is affected by light or dark wallpaper, but it seems that a darker wallpaper might require less power, doesn't it? If so, it probably doesn't have a large effect, so choose a wallpaper that you enjoy viewing.

Picture Frame

Your iPad is capable of being transformed into the most expensive picture frame available, displaying an image from the Photos app on screen for a short period of time before replacing it with another in a slideshow fashion.

Tap Picture Frame in the Settings List and you find a handful of settings that you can tweak on the right side of the screen as shown in Figure 2.15.

FIGURE 2.15   Use your iPad to display a slideshow.

You can choose between a Dissolve and Origami transition. Each transition replaces the on-screen image with the next using a slightly different bit of animation.

Use the Show Each Photo For option to configure the time to display an image on screen in seconds—2, 3, 5, 10, or 20 seconds are your choices.

At the time this lesson was being written, the Zoom in on Faces option was not yet enabled by Apple. But by the time you read this, the service will likely be turned on. If you leave the Zoom in on Faces option set to On, your iPad attempts to identify faces in photographs and zooms in a bit (slowly), which is a nice effect.

You can turn on and off the Shuffle feature; toggling the button to the On position randomly shuffles the images in the Gallery.

And finally, if you choose the All Photos option (unchecked in Figure 2.15), all images are included in the slideshow. Tap the Albums button and select a specific album of photos (Vacation 2011) if you want to show only a subset of the photos stored in the Gallery app. (The Photos app is covered in Lesson 11, in which you learn about organizing images using Albums.)

Oh, and to turn on a slideshow? Easy! Tap the Power/Sleep button to put your iPad to sleep. Tap it again to wake it, but instead of sliding your finger to unlock, tap the small icon that looks like a flower to the right of the slider bar.

General

The General item in the Settings List contains a large number of configurable items, many more than I have room to cover in this lesson. I want to introduce you to a few that I feel are important, but you really should investigate all of these options when you have time to see what they have to offer.

Figure 2.16 shows the setting options after you tap the General option. (Please note that there are a few off-screen options at the bottom that you can only see if you use a swipe gesture to scroll the screen up.)

The settings here are ones related to how the iPad functions as a whole. For example, the About option (refer to Figure 2.16) provides you with details on how much free storage space your iPad currently possesses, its serial number, how many applications, videos, and songs are stored on it, and technical details such as its Wi-Fi and Bluetooth addresses, which are useful to tech support folks.

I mentioned in Lesson 1 that you could change the Mute button so that it becomes a Lock Rotation button. You do that in the General settings. In Figure 2.16 a check mark appears to the right of the Mute option, but in Figure 2.17 you can see that I selected Lock Rotation. Now that button, when turned on (pushed down), prevents my screen from rotating automatically when I turn my iPad 90 degrees or more.

You can control multitasking gestures (covered in Lesson 1) here, as well as set the Auto-Lock time. You see in Figure 2.17 that I've got the Auto-Lock time set to 10 minutes; after 10 minutes of inactivity (no touching the screen, mainly), the iPad automatically goes into Sleep mode. I can turn on the Passcode Lock option and choose a numeric password to prevent unauthorized access to my iPad. (An additional option with the Passcode Lock deletes all data after 10 failed attempts to unlock the code—use this setting at your own risk.)

Again, there is simply too much in the General options to cover in this lesson, but trust me that it's going to be difficult to do anything that cannot be undone. But there is one exception.

About option

FIGURE 2.16   The General settings for your iPad.

Auto-Lock

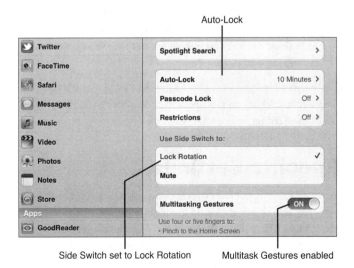

Side Switch set to Lock Rotation   Multitask Gestures enabled

FIGURE 2.17   Changing the Mute button to the Lock Rotation button.

At the very bottom of the General options is the Reset option. If you click it, you see a list of options like those in Figure 2.18.

FIGURE 2.18   The Reset button is not to be toyed with.

From this screen, you can reset your iPad to factory settings, basically erasing it so that it is just like opening the box and starting over. There are buttons that allow you to reset things such as the Home screen layout and the built-in dictionary (removing any words you've added). But these buttons are buried in the same place as the dangerous buttons that reset all settings...so I'm hesitant to have you poking around here. You know it's there, but try to steer clear of it, okay?

Again, I highly encourage you to read over the iPad's User Guide found in the Safari app—it has details on just about every aspect of your iPad, including all of the Settings options and what they do.

App-Specific Settings

Throughout the rest of this book, I cover specific apps that come with your iPad, showing you how to use them and highlighting some of the not-so-obvious features they offer. Many apps, especially the ones that you download from the App Store (see Lesson 7 provide you the ability to configure their settings inside the app, which means you open and run the app and use a menu or button to make changes and tweak settings.

But for many of the apps that come pre-installed with your iPad, you change settings not from within the app, but from the Settings app.

Take a look at Figure 2.19. Below the General option are 12 other items that you can select. They include iCloud, FaceTime, Photos, and GoodReader. You might see a few items in Figure 2.19 that do not appear in your list. Updates to the iPad's operating system might add or take away from the items you see listed, and apps that you choose to download and install appear under the Apps listing such as the GoodReader app that I've already purchased and installed on my iPad.

I mention the GoodReader app to show you an example of an app that can be configured using the Settings app. But the GoodReader app also has options that can only be tweaked by opening and running the app. You should make it a habit of always checking the Settings app after installing an app (from the App Store) to see if there are any settings specific to that app located there. Sometimes you see the app listed in the Settings List...

FIGURE 2.19   Configure additional apps in the Settings app.

sometimes you won't. If you do, tap it and check to see what options are available for the newly installed app.

In addition to learning about the apps that you download and install from the App Store, you should also familiarize yourself with those options specific to the pre-installed apps, such as the Mail app, the Calendar app, the Safari app, and the rest that you see listed in Figure 2.18.

Some of these Settings options won't make sense to you until you learn a bit more about the relevant app. I do my best to point you back to those Settings options that can be important in their respective lessons.

Other Settings options might not even be visible, depending on your make and model of iPad. For example, I have a Wi-Fi only version of the iPad 2, so my Settings List doesn't show the Cellular item—typically sandwiched between the Notifications and Locations Services items—where I would configure information specific to a mobile carrier (such as T-Mobile, AT&T, or Verizon) that offers 3G data service. Again, in these instances, your best bet is to consult the iPad User Guide to learn about those Settings options that are not covered in these lessons but that are important to you.

Summary

In this lesson you had an introduction to the Settings app. The number of options available in the app are too numerous to cover in one lesson, but hopefully you now have a solid understanding of how to navigate the Settings app, how to make changes, and how to check for new settings for your newly downloaded apps.

LESSON 3

Accessing the Internet

In this lesson, you learn about one of the primary functions that the iPad was designed to perform. You learn how to browse the internet, create bookmarks, organize your bookmarks, and use Tabs. You also learn about the AutoFill feature.

The Portable Browser

When the iPad was announced, it was frequently discussed as being a tool for accessing *content*—email, websites, video, and music. The portability of the iPad meant that users could gain access to all of these things and more without the hassle of lugging around a heavy laptop.

The success of the iPad is likely related to many factors, but when you see users carrying iPads out and about, they're usually using it to read a book, listen to music, or watch a video. I rarely see people using the iPad to write the next great novel. I'm not saying it can't be used for that purpose, but the device definitely seems to have a primary role of content provider, whatever that content might be.

Throughout the rest of this book, you learn how to put your iPad to work in a variety of ways, but this lesson focuses on one of the easiest and most basic functions the iPad offers—access to the web. At its most basic level, the iPad makes web browsing more relaxing, enabling you to access the internet from the comfort of your own couch, a booth at your favorite restaurant, or even while waiting for your plane to begin boarding. And it all starts with Safari, the built-in web browser app shown in Figure 3.1.

Start by opening up the Safari app using the icon shown in Figure 3.1.

FIGURE 3.1 The Safari app icon on your iPad.

The Safari app is, by default, placed on your iPad's Dock, but you can move the app (see Lesson 1, "Your iPad 2 Overview") to any Home screen that you like. A single tap on the icon opens Safari, and the last page you were browsing is displayed. Figure 3.2 shows the last webpage I was viewing before I closed Safari—a biography of Jules Verne on www. wikipedia.com.

FIGURE 3.2 Safari saves the last webpage I was viewing.

When you open Safari, you find that the majority of the iPad's touchscreen is dedicated to presenting the webpage you are browsing; you won't find a lot of toolbars and buttons stealing valuable screen space. And rather than a scroll bar on the right-side of the screen as with most web browsers (such as Firefox or Internet Explorer), you use a finger to drag a webpage up and down (or left and right in some instances) to scroll.

> TIP: **Basic Web Browsing Skills**
>
> The purpose of this lesson isn't to teach you about the internet or how it works. If words such as bookmark, hyperlink, and web address are new to you then I recommend you check out *Sams Teach Yourself the Internet in 24 Hours*, 6th Edition to learn more about how the internet works and how a web browser is used to access information.

Let's start with the basics of navigating with Safari before diving into some of the extra features. Learning to use Safari is fast and easy.

Safari Basics

After opening Safari, take a look at the bar that runs across the very top of the screen (whether in Horizontal or Vertical View). The bar has only a few items, which helps limit the size of the bar and gives you more viewable area.

Figure 3.3 shows the toolbar's buttons if you only have one webpage open. (I show you how the toolbar changes when you open multiple webpages in just a moment.)

FIGURE 3.3   The basic Safari toolbar.

From left to right, you find the following:

▶ **Back button**—When you click a hyperlink on the current website, Safari jumps to the new webpage. Tap the Back button once to return to the previous page.

▶ **Forward button**—If you've used the Back button to go back to a previous webpage, the Forward button becomes available and enables you to jump forward (one or more jumps) without having to click the hyperlink again. (This is useful when you want to go back to the start of a web search and work your way through a series of links you've tapped without having to remember the path you took.)

▶ **Bookmarks button**—This button displays webpages that you have chosen to save as bookmarks as well as helps organize your web searches and view browsing history. (More on this later in the lesson.)

▶ **URL Action button**—Tapping the URL Action button calls up a list of options that are applicable to the current web address seen in the Address Field to the right of the button. This button is discussed in more detail later in this lesson.

▶ **URL field**—This is where you enter the web address that you want to visit with Safari. Safari doesn't require that you type in "www" before a web address, so feel free to skip it.

NOTE: **Built-in Reader**

On some web pages (such as the one shown in Figure 3.2), you might see a small Reader button added inside the URL/Webpage Address Field. Tapping this button displays much of the webpage you are currently viewing without the sidebars and other distractions, turning the page into a page that more resembles reading a book or magazine article. Hyperlinks are more subtle (a darker blue) but still functional; tapping a hyperlink takes you to the new page and turns off the Reader function, however.

▶ **Refresh**—At the very end of the URL field is a small circular arrow. This is Safari's Refresh button and you use it to reload the current webpage you are viewing. This is useful when you're visiting a website that has its content updated (refreshed) frequently, such as on websites that provide sports scores, weather reports, and financial information.

▶ **Search Bar**—To the far right of the Safari toolbar is the Google search bar where, when tapped, it enables you to enter one or more keywords using the on-screen keyboard shown in

Figure 3.4; tap the Search button (on the keyboard) and a Google results page is displayed. (By default, Google is the search engine your iPad first uses, but you can change this—see below.)

FIGURE 3.4   The On-screen keyboard.

NOTE: **Change the Search Engine**
You're not locked into using Google as your search tool. Your iPad also offers you Yahoo! and Bing as search engines for the search bar. To change your search tool, open the Settings app (see Lesson 2, "Your iPad's Settings") and tap the Safari app icon in the Settings List running down the left side of the screen. Tap the chevron icon (the right-pointing arrow) in the Search Engine option (on the right side of the screen) and select Bing or Yahoo!.

You can also use the Search Bar to find a keyword on the current page. When the on-screen keyboard is displayed, tap in the Find on Page text box shown in Figure 3.5 and enter your keyword. The first instance of your word (if it exists) is high-lighted. Use the left/right arrow buttons to the right of the text field to move to the previous or next instance of the keyword, respectively.

If you enter a web address incorrectly or want to clear the current web address displayed in the Address Field, tap it once to see the Delete button appear as shown in Figure 3.6. Tap the Delete button and the URL is removed from the Address Field.

Found word

Search on Page for keyword

FIGURE 3.5   Searching for keywords on the current webpage.

Delete button

FIGURE 3.6   Deleting a URL from the Address field.

Copying Text and Images

If you find a bit of text or an image that you want to copy, the iPad makes it easy to grab and store that information. Let's look at copying text first.

Tap and hold your finger to a word (not a hyperlink). A small magnifying glass appears as shown in Figure 3.7 and, when you lift your finger, the word is selected (indicated by the blue highlighting that covers the word).

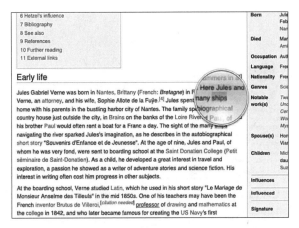

FIGURE 3.7   Select a word on the page to copy.

When you lift your finger, two buttons display just above the word you have selected—Copy and Define. Tapping the Define button opens a small window containing a dictionary definition of the word. After reading the definition, simply tap anywhere else on the screen to close the definition window.

If you tap the Copy button, the word is temporarily stored on the iPad's clipboard, a hidden tool that enables you to cut, copy, and paste text between apps. (You see more examples of this feature in later lessons.)

But what if you want to copy more than a single word? Easy enough. When you select one word, two blue dots appear—one in the upper-left corner of the word and the other in the lower-right corner. Tap and drag one of these dots to select the other words you want to select. (You can select an entire paragraph or even an entire page of text with this method.)

Figure 3.8 shows that I selected a bit of text from the Wikipedia article. After selecting the text, the Copy button is still visible but the Define button has been removed.

If you find an image you want to save, tap and hold your finger on the image. A list of options appears as shown in Figure 3.9, from which you can choose the Save Image or Copy option.

FIGURE 3.8   Select text to copy by dragging the dots with your finger.

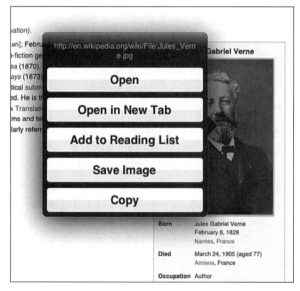

FIGURE 3.9   Tap and hold an image to save or copy it.

Copying Hyperlinks

Sometime you might discover a website that you'd like to return to one day, and your iPad makes it easy to copy and store the web address (also called a URL). As you would with a bit of text or an image, press and hold your finger to a hyperlink until you see a list of options appear (see Figure 3.10).

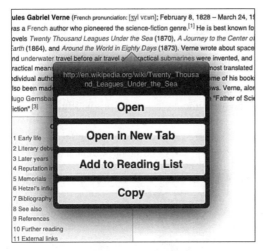

FIGURE 3.10   Hyperlink option available with a finger tap.

Clicking the Open button simply opens that hyperlink and replaces the existing webpage you are viewing. Tapping Open in New Tab opens the website as a separate webpage within Safari (using a feature called Tabs, covered in the next section). Tap Add to Reading List to access it later, or select Copy to copy the URL for pasting into an email message, a note (see Lesson 6), or another app.

Tabs

Okay, you've heard me mention Tabs and the ability to open a new webpage without losing the existing one. You do this using a Safari feature called Tabs, which you can see in action in Figure 3.11.

FIGURE 3.11   Tabs allow multiple webpages to be open at once.

In Figure 3.11, you see that I have three webpages open: a Jules Verne bio, a write-up on *Around the World in 80 Days*, and a write-up on *20,000 Leagues Under the Sea*. Only one webpage can be viewed at a time on the iPad's screen, and in Figure 3.11 I have the Jules Verne bio open.

But with a single tap of my finger on either of the other two tabs, I can immediately view a new webpage without closing the original Jules Verne bio. (See Figure 3.12.)

Currently viewing this tab

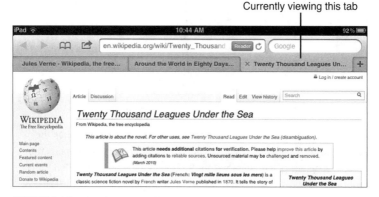

FIGURE 3.12   Another tab selected and its content displayed.

The currently viewed tab is slightly lighter in color than any other tab and a small X appears to the right of the tab's title. You can tap the X to close the tab.

Finally, to create a new tab (and enter a web address manually), tap the + to the far right of the tab bar shown in Figure 3.12. An untitled webpage opens in which you can enter a web address.

Bookmarks

Let's return to the toolbar for a moment and examine the Bookmarks button. When you tap the Bookmarks button, you see a list of options appear like the ones shown in Figure 3.13.

FIGURE 3.13 The Bookmarks button is a useful tool.

Bookmarks are a fundamental tool of web browsers; they enable you to store your favorite websites or set aside newly discovered webpages for later reading. If you choose to use bookmarks, you quickly discover that it pays to apply a little organization to the list.

Refer to Figure 3.13 to see that I have four bookmarks already listed: Apple's website, Google's webpage, the Yahoo! site, and the iPad User Guide, which is stored on the iPad and is accessible via the Safari app.

The other three options at the top of the list in Figure 3.13 are Reading List, History, and Bookmarks Bar.

I already mentioned the Reading List; tap the small chevron to the right and you see a list of all the URLs and webpages that you saved off to the Reading List (using the methods mentioned in the previous sections). This list includes webpages as well as images you might have saved to the Reading List.

The History button displays a list of the most recent seven webpages you visited, as well as options that save browsing history based on date as shown in Figure 3.14.

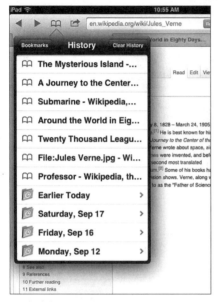

FIGURE 3.14   History can help you find that forgotten web address.

Notice also in Figure 3.14 that you can click the Clear History button to delete the list. When it gets close to my wife's birthday, I tend to use this button quite a bit so she can't see the possible gifts I'm considering. You might have other reasons to hide your tracks, and that's how you do it.

NOTE: **Turn off History Completely**

If you want to disable Safari's ability to track your web browsing history, open the Settings app and click on the Safari icon. Under the Privacy section (on the right side of screen), tap the toggle button to turn On the Private Browsing feature.

Bookmarks make it easy to visit a website with a couple of taps instead of typing a URL in the web address field. Still, after you have a few dozen or more bookmarks created, you want to start organizing them, and for that you use the Edit button shown in Figure 3.13.

After clicking the Edit button, you can delete an existing bookmark by clicking the – (the minus sign in a red dot) to the left of a bookmark as seen in Figure 3.15. Click the New Folder button to create and name a folder such as "Jules Verne" to store bookmarks related to your folder's title.

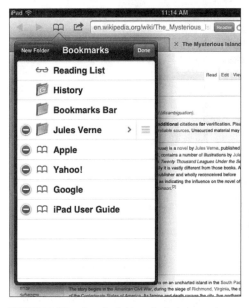

FIGURE 3.15   Create folders to help organize your bookmarks.

Create as many folders as you need to properly organize your growing list of bookmarks. Next I show you how to save webpage bookmarks into those folders.

URL Action Button

Tap on the URL Action button to see a menu like the one in Figure 3.16.

Most of these buttons are fairly self-explanatory. You're already familiar with the Add to Reading List button which, when tapped, adds the website you are currently viewing to the Reading List.

FIGURE 3.16   The URL Action button.

Tapping the Add Bookmark page enables you to enter a title for the bookmark as well as select a folder to place it in. In Figure 3.17, I shortened the title of the current webpage (currently titled "Submarine - Wikipedia, the free encyclopedia") to "Wikipedia - Submarines." I can also tap the chevron to the right of Bookmarks and select the "Jules Verne" folder (or any existing folder) to store the bookmark.

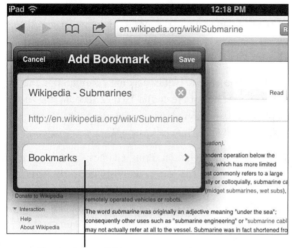

Tap to choose folder

FIGURE 3.17 Rename a bookmark or place it in a folder.

Click the Save button to save your changes or click the Cancel button to stop the bookmarking action.

Returning to the URL Action Button, the Add to Home Screen button is a nice feature that creates an icon (on the first available Home screen with a free slot) that looks like a regular app. Tapping the icon (see Figure 3.18) launches Safari and opens the webpage you selected. You might choose this feature for those websites that you frequent daily (or even hourly) to save yourself the time of hunting through your bookmarks or typing in a URL over and over again.

FIGURE 3.18 You can create shortcuts to websites on a Home screen.

The Mail Link to this Page opens the Mail app (covered in Lesson 4, "Using Email") and enables you to email a shortcut to the webpage. All you need is to know the recipient's email address or have it stored in your Contacts (which is covered in Lesson 6).

The Tweet option works if you have a Twitter account configured in the Settings app. If you haven't set up (or created) a Twitter account, the first time you click this option you are offered the opportunity to install it. I cover Twitter in Lesson 13 and FaceTime in Lesson 9.

And the last item in the URL Action button, Print, enables you to print to any AirPrint-compatible printer that can join your Wi-Fi network. AirPrint enables you to use the wireless capabilities of your iPad to print emails, photos, webpages, PDF files, and more to a supported printer. Not all printers can join a Wi-Fi network, so check your printer's documentation to know for sure.

> NOTE: **AirPrint Tech Support**
>
> Apple has an article that maintains a current list of printers that support AirPrint. You can read that article by opening Safari and entering support.apple.com/kb/HT4356 in the URL field.

Much More to Safari

I didn't have room in this lesson to include everything you need to know about Safari. For example, did you know you can watch embedded videos (such as YouTube videos) that are included on a webpage?

You can also choose to have personal information such as your name, address, and phone number automatically entered into online forms such as e-commerce websites. This feature is called AutoFill, and you can enable it by opening the Settings app, tapping the Safari app in the Settings List, and then tapping the AutoFill toggle button on the right side of the screen.

You must have your personal information stored in the Contacts app (see Lesson 6), but after it's stored, your iPad offers you a button like the one in Figure 3.19 when providing specific types of information is necessary. Tapping the button automatically fills in those areas that you have stored in the Contacts app. Cool, huh?

AutoFill
button

FIGURE 3.19   AutoFill saves time and typing.

If you want to learn more about Safari and its features, the best way to do it is with the actual Safari app. Just tap the Bookmarks button, select iPad User Guide, and then tap any icon that you want to know more about (such as the Safari app) or use the Quick Search tool indicated in Figure 3.20 to type in a keyword to narrow your search. This tool not only works when you need help with Safari, but with any of the apps you see listed down the left side of Figure 3.20.

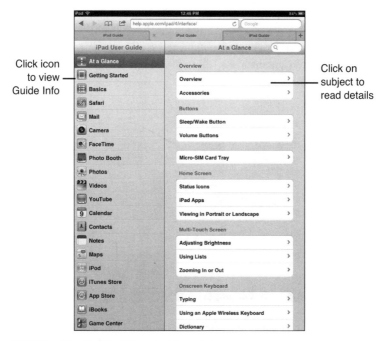

Click icon to view Guide Info

Click on subject to read details

FIGURE 3.20   The iPad User Guide in Safari.

Summary

In this lesson you were introduced to Safari, the iPad's default web browser. You learned how Safari displays websites, including how it handles opening multiple web pages using tabs. You learned about bookmarks and how to create and organize them to make browsing and finding what you need quicker and easier.

LESSON 4
Using Email

In this lesson, you learn about the iPad's Mail app and how to read, send, and organize your email messages. You also learn how to set up an email account, send attachments, change your email signature, and more.

The Mail App

After web browsing, email is the next most popular activity that users report for their iPads. (You can view the entire survey conducted by *Business Insider* by visiting http://www.businessinsider.com/how-people-really-use-the-ipad-our-exclusive-survey-results-2011-5.) Email has become a key component of our lives, and it's no surprise to find that Apple has provided a built-in app called Mail that is perfect for tablet users.

Most people have become accustomed to a large number of bells and whistles included with their email applications. But the Mail app is fairly thin on special features; its streamlined approach to managing email (both sending and receiving) goes hand in hand with the portable nature of the iPad. There are certainly other email apps available if you find that you need an email feature that's not included with Mail.

However, before you go hunting down a new email app, give Mail a try. You might find that it can do everything you need (and perhaps a little more). The first thing you need to do to use the Mail app is set up an email account. Tap the Mail icon shown in Figure 4.1 to get started.

FIGURE 4.1   The Mail app icon on your iPad.

Because your iPad doesn't have an email account already configured, you need to select the option (see Figure 4.2) that corresponds to your email provider.

FIGURE 4.2   Select a button that works for your email address.

If you use Gmail, for example, tap the Gmail button. If you're an AOL user, tap the AOL button. If you're a user of Apple's MobileMe or iCloud services, and your email address ends with @me.com, select either of those options. The Microsoft Exchange button helps you configure an email account that is hosted by an Exchange Server (most likely a company provided email address), and the Other button enables you to provide details about other email accounts such as an address provided to you by your Internet Service Provider (ISP).

> TIP: **You Might Need to Provide Special Information**
>
> For the Gmail, Hotmail, Yahoo!, MobileMe, iCloud, and AOL options, all you need to provide is your email address and password, which is information you already know. For the Microsoft Exchange and Other options, you probably need to provide additional information that is typically only obtained from the IT department (the techie crew) at your company or from your ISP. If you need additional assistance with configuring the Mail app for your email address, contact the tech support team that handles your email (either a department in your company or possibly your ISP).

I walk you through setting up a Gmail account here, but the steps are pretty much identical for AOL, Yahoo!, Hotmail, and MobileMe/iCloud users. I'm assuming you already have an email account created somewhere. If you don't, feel free to visit http://mail.google.com and use the Create an Account link to sign up for a free Gmail account.

Configure an Account

Tap the Gmail button (refer to Figure 4.2), and you see a screen like the one in Figure 4.3. I've already filled out the four fields (Name, Address, Password, and Description) with my own email info, so keep in mind it won't match yours.

FIGURE 4.3   Provide basic info for your email account.

Tap the Next button and the Mail app attempts to verify the account by checking the password. If you entered the information correctly, you are prompted to turn On or Off the Calendar and Notes integration as seen in Figure 4.4. The Calendar app and the Notes app that come with your iPad have the ability to import appointments from your Gmail Calendar and notes from your Gmail account. I recommend that you leave them set to On to keep this information synchronized with your Google account, but you can easily turn them off if you don't want your Google account information saved to your iPad.

FIGURE 4.4 Gmail settings for use with the Email app.

Keep in mind that your email address might not have a calendar or notes feature that integrates with the iPad, so don't worry if you don't have this option.

Next, tap the Save button and your account saves to the iPad. The Mail app opens.

NOTE: **Mail Will Synchronize with Your Email Account**
You might see a few messages displayed in Mail or you might see a lot. It just depends on how many email messages you have already waiting to be viewed.

Now that the Mail app is open and you have an email address setup for use with your iPad, let's take a look at how easy it is to send and for receiving messages. For the remainder of this lesson, rotate your iPad to Horizontal View. Keep in mind that you can view the Mail app in Vertical View, but the Horizontal View enables you to view your folders (such as Inbox, Trash/Deleted, and Drafts) on the left side of the screen as well as an open email message on the right side of the screen.

Checking for Messages

After rotating the iPad to Horizontal View, my Mail app displays a list of my folders down the left side as shown in Figure 4.5.

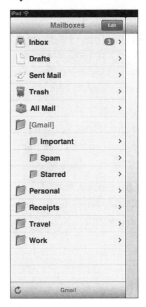

FIGURE 4.5   Folders are displayed down the left side of the screen.

If you don't see the list of folders but instead see a list of email messages like the screen shown in Figure 4.6, tap the Mailboxes button to return to the list of folders.

Mailboxes button

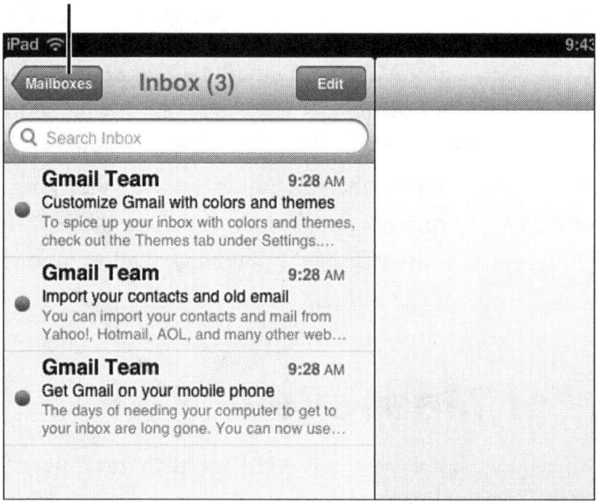

FIGURE 4.6   If the Inbox folder is open, email messages are visible.

When in folder view (refer to Figure 4.5), a single tap of your finger on any folder opens it and displays any email messages stored inside. Figure 4.6, for example, shows the three messages currently in the Inbox folder. The blue dots to the left of each message indicate the email has not yet been read.

If I tap a message stored in a folder (whether it's Inbox, Drafts, or some other folder), the contents of that message are displayed on the right side of the screen as shown in Figure 4.7.

No matter which folder you have open, if you tap the Refresh button indicated in Figure 4.7, the Mail app checks for any new messages that have been sent to you. You can tap the Refresh button at any time.

Refresh button

FIGURE 4.7 Tap a message to view its contents.

NOTE: **Change the Default Time to Check for Messages**

The Mail app is capable of receiving email that is *pushed* out by your mail service, but not all mail services do this. In order to have the Mail app check for you, open the Settings app, tap on the Mail, Contacts, Calendar option in the Settings List, tap the Fetch New Data option, and turn off the Push feature by tapping the toggle button to turn it Off. After the Push feature is turned off, select a time (Every 15 Minutes, Every 30 Minutes, Hourly, or Manually) and Mail checks for mail based on your selection. Note that the Manually option means you always need to tap the Refresh button to check for new email.

As new email arrives, it is delivered to your Inbox. Exceptions to this rule do exist, and some email providers such as Google's Gmail are capable of flagging email as Spam and automatically routing it to the Spam folder.

When new messages are sent to the Inbox, a small number indicating the number of unread email messages appears to the right of the Inbox (see Figure 4.8).

FIGURE 4.8   The number of unread email messages in my Inbox.

Replying to an Email

After you read an email, you can choose to reply to, forward, or print it by tapping the arrow indicating the Action button in Figure 4.9. A list of options displays.

Actions button

FIGURE 4.9   Tap the Action button to select an action.

If the message only has one sender and one recipient, you only see the Reply option. For emails with multiple recipients, you also see a Reply to All option.

Tap the Reply button to see a screen like the one in Figure 4.10. Type your response in the top of the message. You can also see in the figure that the original message is appended to the end of your new email, the sender's email address is placed in the To: box, and "Re:" is added to the Subject line text.

Forwarding a message is just as easy. Select the Forward option to enter your own text above the original message. The To: field is left blank so you can enter the recipient's address as shown in Figure 4.11. Note the + button to the right of the To: field. Tap it to display your Contacts (see Lesson 6, "Working with Notes, Messages, and Contacts") and select one (or more) rather than typing in the email address with the onscreen keyboard.

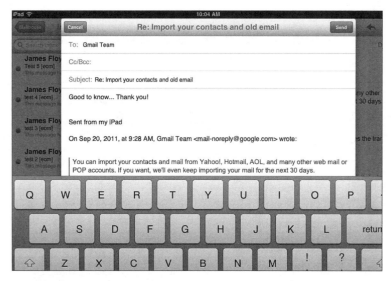

FIGURE 4.10   Replying to an email is simple.

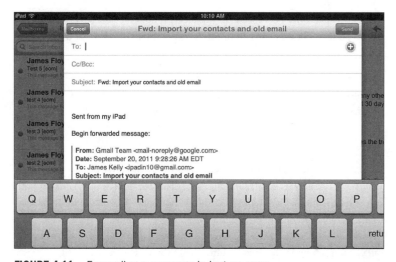

FIGURE 4.11   Forwarding a message is just as easy.

Finally, selecting the Print option enables you to print the email message if you have a printer that supports AirPrint (refer to Lesson 3, "Accessing the Internet").

Sending an Email

You have now seen how to read, reply to, print, and forward existing email messages, but how do you compose your own email? Whether you view your list of folders or have an email message open to read, you can always click the Compose button (see Figure 4.12) to begin typing a new message.

You can then create your email message as shown in Figure 4.13. As with the Forward option, you can click the + button to the right of the To: field to select recipients from your Contacts list or you can type in the email address directly.

Compose button ┐

FIGURE 4.12   Tap the Compose button to type an email message.

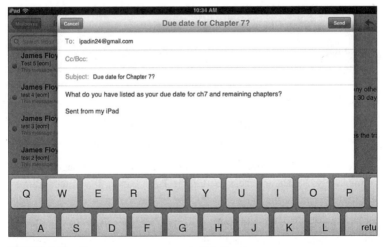

FIGURE 4.13   Type your message and click Send.

Type in a bit of text for the Subject line, type your main email message, and tap the Send button in the upper-right corner! If the sound is turned up enough on your iPad, you hear a slight whooshing sound that indicates the message was sent.

NOTE: **The Signature Line**
You might have noticed in Figure 4.13 the "Sent from my iPad" signature line that is added automatically to the end of any new email message you send. You can change the text or turn off that feature completely by opening the Settings app, tapping the Mail, Contacts, Calendars option, and then tapping the Signature feature. Simply change the text with the onscreen keyboard or delete it altogether.

Organize Your Email

Now that you know how to compose messages, check for new emails, and read and reply, you should know how to manage your email so you don't have to sift through hundreds or thousands of messages to find an email of interest. To do this, you need to know how to quickly archive messages or send them to the trash, for example.

Take a look at Figure 4.14. One of the email messages from the Gmail Team is open on the right side of the screen. It's been read and is no longer needed, so it belongs in the Trash folder. To do this, tap on the Folder Select button.

After you tap the Folder Select button, the message shrinks slightly and you see the folders on the left side of the screen as shown in Figure 4.15.

Simply tap a folder on the left side of the screen and the message is moved immediately. To delete a message, tap the Trash button. If you tap a different folder's button, the message is moved to that folder.

One useful folder is the All Mail folder. This folder, when selected, displays all messages stored in all your folders minus the Trash and Spam folders. It's just a quick way to view all your messages, no matter how you've organized them. It also holds archived mail that you no longer want stored in your Inbox but don't want to delete. To archive a message, simply tap the Archive button when you read a message as shown in Figure 4.16.

Folder Select button

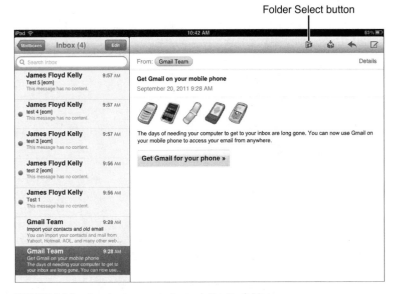

FIGURE 4.14   Send a message to a particular folder.

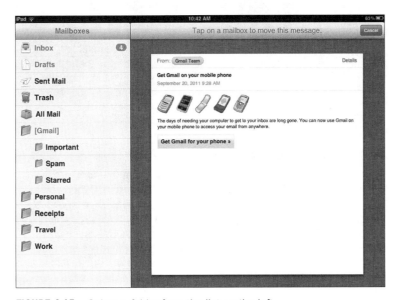

FIGURE 4.15   Select a folder from the list on the left.

Edit button   Archive button

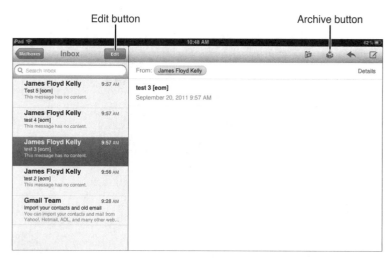

FIGURE 4.16   Archive a message to save it.

NOTE: **The Delete Button May Appear**

For most email providers (other than Google's Gmail), the All Mail button changes to a garbage can icon. Tap that button to immediately delete the message. And if you use Gmail, you can get the Delete icon rather than the All Mail option when you disable archiving in the Settings app. To do this, tap Settings, then the Mail, Contacts, Calendars option, then tap the Gmail item on the right side of the screen and turn the Archive Messages toggle button to Off.

NOTE: **Shortcut to Archive a Message**

Rather than opening a message and then tapping the Archive button to send it to the All Mail folder, there is a shortcut. When you have a list of email messages displayed on the left (after tapping a folder to open it), simply slide your finger over the message and an Archive button appears. Tap the button to send the message immediately to the All Mail folder or slide your finger again to remove the button and cancel the archive action.

Look at Figure 4.17; you might notice that there's a new folder called
Writing in the list on the left. This is a folder I created. You can create
your own folders, too, by tapping the Edit button indicated in Figure 4.16.

FIGURE 4.17   Create a new folder to store email messages.

After tapping the Edit button, click the New Mailbox button at the very
bottom of the list (see Figure 4.17).

Enter a name for the folder using the on-screen keyboard and select where
you want that folder to be stored. If you leave it the default location (in
this instance, Gmail) the folder appears in the master list of folders seen in
all previous screenshots. If you want to make your new folder a subfolder—that is, you want to place it inside an existing folder—then you
have to tap the Mailbox Location chevron (refer to Figure 4.17) and select
the folder where you want the new folder to be created. When you've
established where the new folder should be created, tap the Save button.

FIGURE 4.18   Create a new subfolder.

In Figure 4.19 you can see a newly created folder called Proposals that is inside the Writing folder.

Tap the Done button (seen in Figure 4.17) and your new folder is ready to be used to organize your messages.

FIGURE 4.19   A subfolder and its parent folder.

Much More to Mail

There are many more things you can do with the Mail app, but I've run out of space in this lesson. Remember, you can search the iPad User's Guide stored in the Safari app's Bookmarks menu (refer to Lesson 3) or open the Settings app and tap on the Mail, Contacts, Calendars option to view other settings that you can tweak to customize your experience with the Mail app. As you can see in Figure 4.20, there are many more settings available to you that you can experiment with and read about in the iPad User Guide.

Click to
access Mail
app settings

Mail app
settings
below

FIGURE 4.20   The Settings app offers other options for Mail app users.

Summary

In this lesson you saw how to configure an email account for use with the
Mail app. You also learned how to send, receive, forward, delete, and move
email messages with the Mail app's built-in tools.

LESSON 5

Working with Calendars and Reminders

In this lesson, you learn to use the simple but useful Calendar and Reminder apps. You learn how to set appointments, configure alerts, and create reminders.

The Calendar App

If you carry your iPad with you just about everywhere you go, you might find that using the iPad's Calendar app is a good way to stay organized. I use it to keep track of my conference calls, when my book's chapters are due, and even when to replace the air conditioner filters in my home.

You can enter new items (the iPad Calendar app calls them events) directly into the Calendar app at any time, but if you use Google Calendar you can merge (or synchronize) it with the Calendar app as well. (Refer to Figure 4.4 to see the toggle switch that imports your calendar.)

Take a look at Figure 5.1 to see the Calendar app icon. The icon always displays the numerical day of the month so that's a nice little feature that Apple included for those of us who are always forgetting today's date.

FIGURE 5.1 The Calendar app icon.

Tap the Calendar app to open it, and you are greeted with one of five possible screens: Day, Week, Month, Year, or List. (Calendar saves the current view when you close the app so that view is open when you next launch the app.) In Figure 5.2, Day View is displayed, but a single tap on any of the five buttons changes the view.

FIGURE 5.2   Day View for the Calendar app.

When you first open the Calendar app, you may find event entries from events previously entered in your Google Calendar account. Without even knowing how to create new events in Calendar, you can still modify an existing event. For example, in Figure 5.2, you can see the one event scheduled for the day—Write Chapter 5. It's scheduled from 9:00 a.m. to 5:00 p.m. (You learn how to schedule events in a moment.) You can tap on one of the small dots at the top or bottom edge of the block that represents the event and drag them to adjust the time. Figure 5.3 shows that the event has been adjusted to occur between 10:00 a.m. and 4:00 p.m.

Drag to adjust time

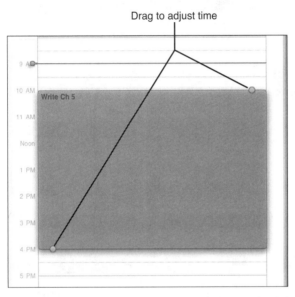

FIGURE 5.3   Modify the schedule by moving a couple of dots.

You can adjust the times manually with the dots in 15 minute increments. You can also tap and hold the block representing the event and drag it up or down if you want the length of the event to stay the same (six hours in this instance) but want the start and end times to change.

> TIP: **Move the Event to a Different Day**
>
> While in Day View, you can press and hold an event block and drag it to the left or right to move it to a previous day or a subsequent day. Continue to drag it to one of the edges to flip through the days (backward or forward), but be aware that the Calendar app flips fast, so you might miss your target and have to drag it back the other direction.

Change Views by tapping on the Week View (refer to Figure 5.2). The screen changes to the one shown in Figure 5.4.

Click to Add Event ⌐

FIGURE 5.4   The Week View shows a bit more information.

With Week View, there is a seven-day summary of the current week. The current day (Thursday the 22nd in the example) is highlighted in blue. Notice at the very bottom of the screen is a series of buttons that enable you to jump to earlier or future weeks.

> NOTE: **Use the Today Button to Jump Quickly to Today**
>
> No matter which view you are using, in the lower-left corner of the screen is the Today button. If you are viewing any Day, Week, or Month that does not currently display today's date, tapping that button immediately changes your current view to the Day, Week, or Month View that displays the current day.

Knowing how to modify an existing event's time and changing the view format is nice, but the Calendar app won't be of much use to you if you don't know how to create a new event. In the bottom-right corner of the screen, tap the + symbol to open the Add Event window and the onscreen keyboard shown in Figure 5.5.

FIGURE 5.5   Creating a new event requires a single tap.

Enter the name of your event (Dentist Appointment, for example). You can also enter a location if you wish.

Next, tap anywhere in the Starts/Ends/TimeZone box (seen in Figure 5.5) and the on-screen keyboard closes as shown in Figure 5.6.

The first thing you set is the day of the event and the start time. Press and hold your finger on the left side of the spinning wheel indicated in Figure 5.6. Moving your finger up turns the wheel and enables you to select a future date (such as Friday, September 23rd). Moving your finger down rotates the wheel down to enable you to select an earlier date.

Perform the same rotating action on the hour and minute wheels. You also turn the right-most wheel to select AM or PM for the event.

Spin to set date/time

FIGURE 5.6   Set the date and time of your event.

After setting the start time, tap the Ends section of the screen and use the same rotating action to set the date and time when the event ends. You can also toggle the All-day button to On if you want to set the event to occur all day without a specific start or end time. Finally, tap the Time Zone chevron to set a different time zone for the event (this is useful if you're scheduling an appointment while you are travelling in a different time zone). When you're done setting the dates and times for the event, tap the Done button.

Figure 5.7 shows a new event that starts on Monday, September 26th, at10:00 a.m. and ends at 1:15 p.m.

In Week View, the Calendar app changes to the week of the event. Similarly, if you choose Day View, it jumps to the day of the new event, as shown in Figure 5.8. Notice that the event has not been confirmed yet. Before tapping the Done button to confirm the event and schedule it in the Calendar app, let's look at a few more options available on the configuration window shown in Figure 5.8.

— Done button

FIGURE 5.7   Set the date and time and tap Done.

Date of appointment

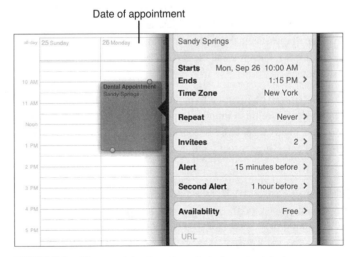

FIGURE 5.8   The event is almost ready to be scheduled.

NOTE: **Shortcut for Creating an Event**
Instead of tapping the + button to create an event, you can tap on the screen on the day and/or time that you want to create an event. This enables you to immediately select the day of the event as well as the start time. A window like the one in Figure 5.7 is provided to you to configure the end time and a few other options.

In Figure 5.8 you can see that there are five new sections that can be configured: Repeat, Invitees, Alert, Calendar, and Availability. There's also an area to enter a URL (web address) and a note (such as a gate code to enter a community or maybe a note that the meeting is business casual).

Tap the Repeat chevron to select the calendar placement of the event you create—Every Day, Every Week, Every 2 Weeks, Every Month, or Every Year. The default is None so that the event is a one-time event, but if you want to create a recurring event, such as a reminder about weekly soccer practice on Tuesdays, set the new event for its Tuesday time and then select the Every Week option. The Calendar app then enters that event every Tuesday.

Tap the Invitees chevron to select one or more contacts from the Contacts app (see Lesson 6, "Working with Notes, Messages, and Contacts") and send them an email message asking them to confirm their attendance. (I show you what happens when someone accepts an invitation to an event later in this chapter.)

Tap the Alert chevron to configure a reminder that appears on the iPad's screen. You can configure this reminder to pop up at the time of the event or up to two days in advance. Even if your iPad is in Sleep mode, the alert turns on the iPad and chirps to get your attention!

TIP: **Create a Second Alert If Necessary**
If you need another reminder for an event, Calendar enables you to configure a second alert as a last-chance reminder.

The Availability option enables you to set an event and shows you as Busy or Free. You might want to use this option to create blocks of free time on your calendar to remind yourself not to schedule anything.

Figure 5.9 shows the example event with all the settings configured. Tap the Done button to add the event to the calendar.

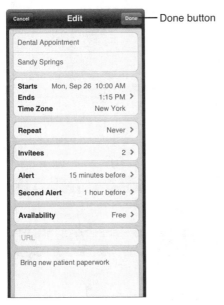

FIGURE 5.9 Tap Done so the event is added to your calendar.

Before finishing up with the Calendar app, take a quick look at the remaining views. Figure 5.10 shows the Month View. This view shows a month's worth of events as well as displaying the start time for each event. Notice that all-day events (such as birthdays) are displayed inside a blue bar with no start time assigned.

Figure 5.11 shows the Year View. Although details are not displayed, all days with at least one event scheduled are indicated with a yellow box on the date. The box gets darker (approaching the color red) as more events are scheduled on a particular day. Tap a box to open and display that day's events in Day View. The current day is indicated by a blue box.

FIGURE 5.10   The Month View in the Calendar app.

FIGURE 5.11   The Year View on the Calendar app.

List View is shown in Figure 5.12. This view is a slightly modified version of the Day View. The current day's schedule is visible on the right side of the screen, and you can view all upcoming events on the scrollable window on the left side of the screen. You can scroll the list of events up or down indefinitely to see years' of events before or after the current date. Tapping an event on the scrollable list changes the Day View on the left side of the screen to that day's view.

FIGURE 5.12   The List View on the Calendar app.

Finally, I mentioned earlier that you can invite people from the Contacts app to an event. All invitees receive an email message like the one in Figure 5.13. They can click the Accept, Decline, or Maybe buttons to send a response to your calendar.

Refer to Figure 5.13 to see that the invitee has accepted (the Yes is solid next to the Going? question), but the Decline and Maybe options are also listed in case an invitee needs to select one of those options. Also notice in the List View that the Notes section displays any comments you add for an event.

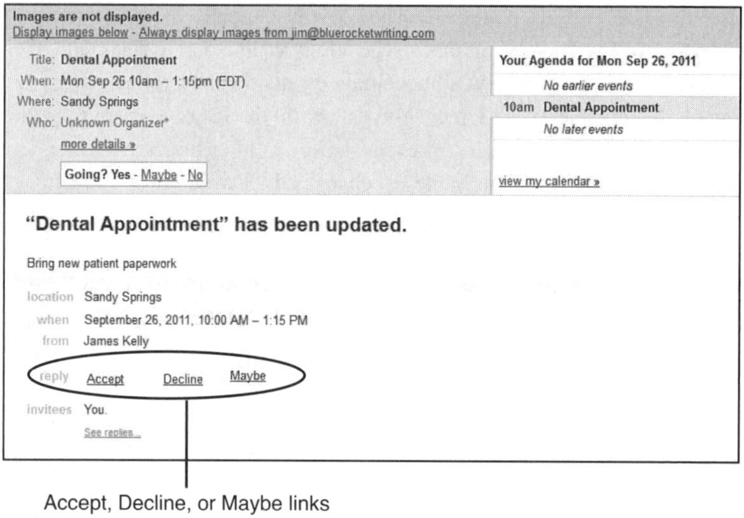

Accept, Decline, or Maybe links

FIGURE 5.13   Invitees can choose to Accept or Decline an invite.

The Calendar app has other capabilities that I don't have space to cover here, so please consult the iPad User Guide by opening the Safari app, tapping on the Bookmarks button, and selecting the iPad User Guide option to learn more about the Calendar app.

Remember to Use Reminders

Although the Calendar app is very useful, you might find that creating events and modifying their settings is more "help" than you actually need from your iPad. If you want an even simpler app that enables you to type out a description of an event and set a quick reminder then the Reminders app might be all you need.

Tap the Reminders app icon (see Figure 5.14) to open the app. You see a screen similar to the one in Figure 5.15. (At first, you may have no reminders listed; there's one shown in the example.)

FIGURE 5.14 The Reminders app icon.

FIGURE 5.15 The Reminders screen is simple and easy to use.

The easiest way to understand Reminders is to create an item. To do this, tap the + button in the upper-right corner. A blinking cursor displays on the screen as shown in Figure 5.16; this is where any text you type is displayed.

After entering the text, tap the Return button on the keyboard and the new reminder is shown in the list (see Figure 5.17).

Simply adding a reminder to the list doesn't do you much good if you don't open the Reminders app and view the list. Fortunately, you can create alerts so the Reminders app will give you a reminder similar to the way an Alert in the Calendar app works.

Cursor for new reminder

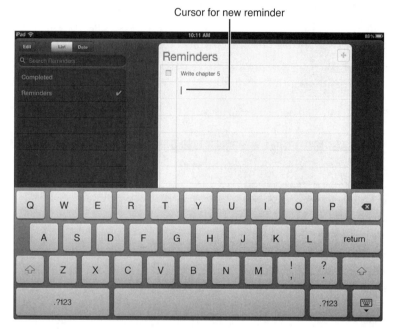

FIGURE 5.16   Type a bit of text for your reminder.

Remind Me chevron

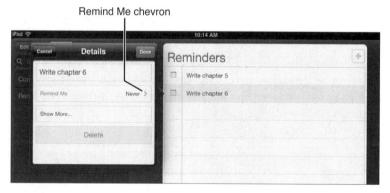

FIGURE 5.17   Your new reminder item is added.

Tap the Remind Me chevron seen in Figure 5.17. A new window displays as shown in Figure 5.18.

Tap the On a Day toggle button to turn it On as shown in Figure 5.18. Tap the date/time section and rotate the wheel to set the date and time that you want the alert to trigger.

Tap to set reminder date/time   Tap to turn ON

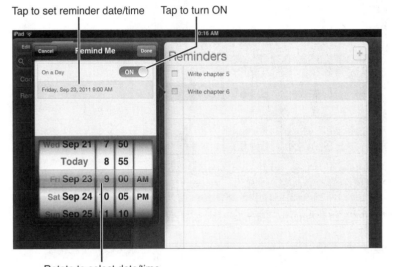

Rotate to select date/time

FIGURE 5.18   You can create alerts for your reminders.

Tap the Done button to set the reminder alert (see Figure 5.20). Click the Show More button and, as with the Calendar app's events, you tap the Repeat chevron shown in Figure 5.20 to set the reminder alert to trigger on a recurring schedule (Every Day or Every 2 Weeks, for example).

If you click the Priority chevron you can set the reminder's priority to None, Low, Medium, and High. Enter any notes you want to associate with the reminder by tapping the Notes section and using the onscreen keyboard.

FIGURE 5.19   Set your reminder alert and click Done.

FIGURE 5.20   Configure more reminder options.

When the reminder's alert is triggered, a window appears on the iPad's screen (see Figure 5.21). The alert even pops up on the screen if the iPad is in Sleep Mode.

FIGURE 5.21 A reminder alert displays on the iPad screen.

One thing you need to be aware of with both the Calendar and the Reminders apps is that any items you enter in one app are not automatically added to the other. It would have been a nice feature to be able to create a reminder and have it automatically added to the calendar (or vice versa) but that might have to wait for a future update.

Summary

In this lesson you were introduced to the Calendar app and the Reminders app. You learned how to add new events and configure special settings such as alerts. You also found out how alerts display on your iPad to keep you informed.

LESSON 6

Working with Notes, Messages, and Contacts

In this lesson, you learn to use three apps: Notes, Contacts, and Messages. You learn how to create and save notes, add and delete contacts, and chat with instant messaging using the Messages app.

Notes

Of all the apps that are preinstalled on your iPad, Notes has to be the simplest to use and also the most intuitive. It's a notepad, but it's a digital version. Instead of hand writing your notes, you type them in with the onscreen keyboard.

To launch the Notes app, tap the Notes icon (see Figure 6.1).

FIGURE 6.1   The Notes app icon on your iPad.

When you open Notes the first time, the top page is blank, as shown in Figure 6.2. Notice that on every page the current date and time display at the top and a simple toolbar with four icons is at the bottom. In the upper-left corner of the screen is a Notes button that, when tapped, opens a list of any existing notes that you've saved.

Notes button

Current date and time

Toolbar

FIGURE 6.2   A new note page using the Notes app.

Figure 6.2 shows the Notes app in Vertical View, but for the rest of this section I use Horizontal View. In Horizontal View you can see not only the current note, but you can also see a list of all other note pages you've created down the left side of the screen (see Figure 6.3).

In Figure 6.3, you can see that the name of the note (New Note) circled on the left in the Notes List. When you type a bit of text on the first line, that text becomes the note's title. In Figure 6.4 New Note has changed to "Office supplies needed."

Any additional text you type below the first line is simply part of the note; you can change the title at any time by editing the first line of the note. Simply tap at the end of the line to place the cursor on the line, and use the backspace key to delete the first line and replace it with a new line (that also becomes the new title).

Notes List   New Note

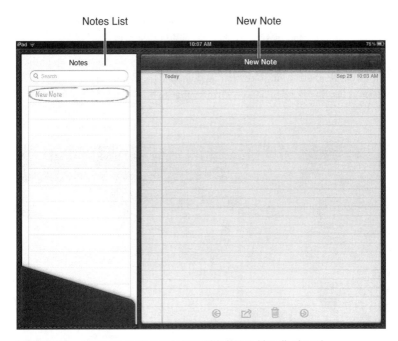

FIGURE 6.3 Notes in Horizontal View with Notes List displayed.

Note title   First line of note

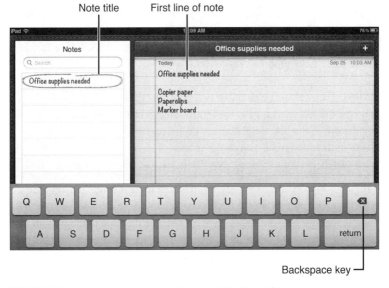

Backspace key

FIGURE 6.4 A note takes its title from the first line of text.

If you want to delete a word, tap twice on the word. The word is high-lighted and you can click the backspace button to delete it.

Deleting an entire line, however, requires one more step. Double-tap at the end of the line you want to remove and choose the Select option. The last word on the line is selected as shown in Figure 6.5.

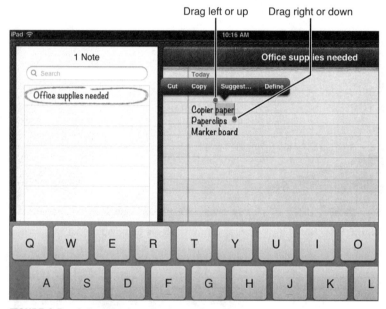

FIGURE 6.5   Select the last word on a line of text.

Use your finger to drag one of the two dots. Drag the dot in the upper-left corner of the selected word to the left to select words to the left. Likewise, drag the dot in the lower-right corner of the selected word to the right to select words to the right. You can drag these dots up or down to select entire sentences or paragraphs above or below the selected word.

In Figure 6.6, Copier Paper is highlighted and several command choices are displayed. You can tap the backspace key to delete the line; for this example, choose the Cut option so you can paste that line at the bottom of the note. You can also select the Copy option to leave the selected words where they are and then use a Paste command to paste the same text else-where in the note.

Cut option   Copy option

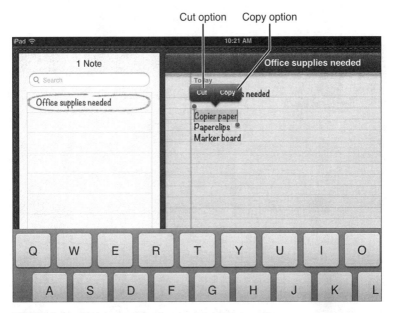

FIGURE 6.6   Select an entire line to delete, Cut, or Copy.

Now that the text is cut, tap to place the cursor at the end of the last line in the note (just after the Marker board item in Figure 6.6) and tap the Enter key to create a new line. Tap on the blank line and choose the Paste option (see Figure 6.7).

To save this note, click the + in the upper-right corner of the Notes app. The note you were working on saves and a blank note page opens.

As you create new notes they appear in the Notes List to the left. (If you're in Vertical View, tap the Notes button in the upper-left corner to toggle the Notes List on and off.)

As your list of notes begins to increase in quantity, it might be difficult to find a particular note or bit of text. When this happens, use the Search bar (see Figure 6.9). As you type a word in the box, the Notes List automatically begins to filter all the notes you have and only displays those that have the search word or words in them.

Paste option

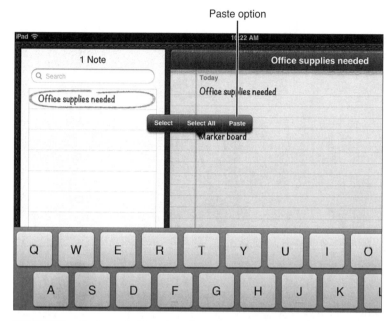

FIGURE 6.7   Paste copied text into the note at a new location.

Tap to create new note ⌐

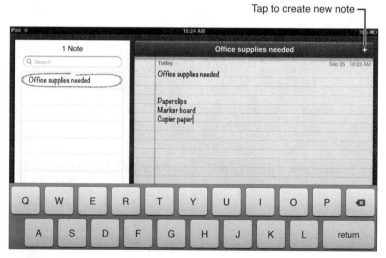

FIGURE 6.8   Create a new note and save the existing one.

Search box

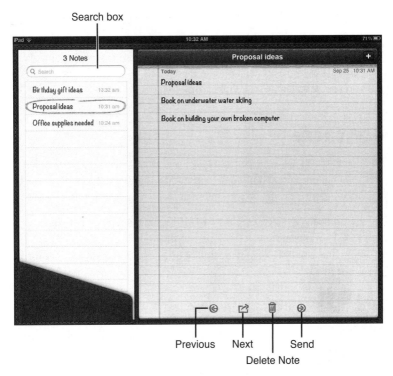

Previous Next Send
Delete Note

FIGURE 6.9 Navigate through your list with Previous and Next buttons.

Take a look at the toolbar at the bottom of any notes page. You see a trash-can icon that's probably easy to figure out; tap it once to delete the current note you are viewing. You are asked to confirm your decision, so tap the Delete Note button if you really want to delete the current note.

Figure 6.9 shows what happens as you view existing notes. The Previous and Next arrows enable you to move forward and backward through your notes list. (When you view the first note in the list, the Previous button won't be available; likewise, viewing the last note in your list disables the Next button.

Finally, tap the Send button indicated in Figure 6.9 to email or print the note. Printing is only available with a printer that supports AirPrint (see Lesson 3, "Accessing the Internet"). The Email option opens the Email app and puts the text of the note into the body of the new email message.

(Refer to Lesson 4, "Using Email," for instructions on sending email messages.)

As your Notes List grows, you can scroll it up and down with a swipe of your finger. You can also tap a note in the Notes List to immediately jump to that note. Next, let's take a look at the Contacts app.

Contacts

The Contacts app is where you store all the mailing addresses, phone numbers, email addresses, and more for those individuals and businesses in your life.

Tap the Contacts app icon (see Figure 6.10) to open the app, and you are presented with a blank screen like the one shown in Figure 6.11. (I'm assuming that you haven't previously imported or entered any of your own contacts.)

FIGURE 6.10   The Contacts app on your iPad.

Tap the + button indicated in Figure 6.11, and a blank contacts form displays as shown in Figure 6.12.

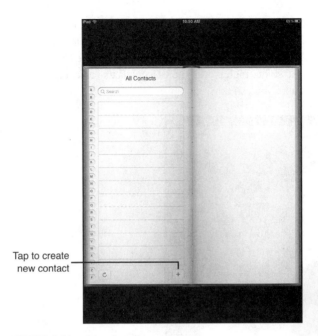

FIGURE 6.11   An empty Contacts list.

Tap to create
new contact

FIGURE 6.12   A blank contacts form for entering information.

This is a scrollable page, so you need to use your finger to move the form up and down the page as needed. Use the onscreen keyboard to enter information such as First Name, Last Name, Company, Phone Number, Email Address, and so on. Figure 6.13 shows a contact's basic information, but there's more you can do.

FIGURE 6.13   A new contact added to the Contacts app.

Some fields, such as the Phone and Email fields, provide an additional area after you type in some text. For example, in the example the Home Email field appeared after I entered the work email address. You can use these new fields or ignore them.

In Figure 6.14 the screen is scrolled down a bit to make available other fields, such as mailing address, notes, and birthday. Tap the + button indicated in Figure 6.14 to add a new field if something you need is missing from the list. (Examples of additional fields include Job Title, Department, Twitter Address, and a few more.)

Tap to delete information

Tap to add new field

FIGURE 6.14   Finishing up a contact's information.

Tap the Done button to save the new contact's information. The new contact is visible in the book (he's the only contact at this point) as shown in Figure 6.15. When you have multiple contacts, you can tap the letter of the name and the Contacts app jumps to those contacts.

When viewing a contact, you can click the Edit button (refer to Figure 6.15) at the bottom of the contact page and make any necessary changes. Scroll to the bottom of the contact page and tap the Delete Contact button if you want to remove the contact completely.

You can tap the Add Photo icon (refer to Figure 6.12) when creating a new contact or while editing a contact's information and choose to either take a photo (with the iPad's built-in camera) or select a photo from the Photos app (see Lesson 11, "Using the Photos App," for more information).

Finally you can import existing contacts from your Gmail account into the Contacts app. It's not difficult to do, but there are more steps than I have room to include in this lesson. Instead, open your Safari browser and visit http://bit.ly/9xmw64 to view the steps complete with screenshots.

Tap letters to jump
to last names

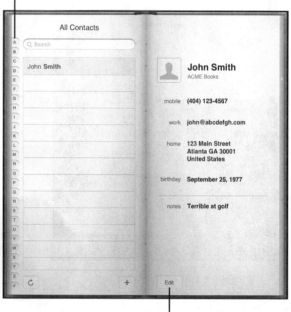

Edit current contact

FIGURE 6.15   A new contact added and visible in the list.

TIP: **Importing Other Contact Databases**

You can do a Google search to find out if it's possible to import other types of contact databases into your iPad. There are so many varieties of contact databases that it's impossible to say for certain whether they can be imported or not. I suggest doing an internet search for the name of your contact database application or the type of database and include "import to iPad" as part of the keyword phrase.

Messages

If you're familiar with instant messaging then you understand the Messages app easily enough. If instant messaging is new to you, the best explanation I can offer is to think of instant messaging like a phone call but instead of talking, you type your conversation.

When you're on a phone call, both parties can talk at once, but it doesn't make for an easy-to-understand call, does it? The same is true for instant messaging; while you type that long two or three-sentence message, the other person can type a message, too. If that happens, you might find that you ask a question or send a message that interrupts the flow of the conversation. Many instant messaging fans develop a habit of sending a message and then waiting for a response... a back-and-forth text conversation.

Your iPad supports instant messaging with the Messages app, but you need to turn it on first. Open the Settings app and tap the Messages item in the Settings List as shown in Figure 6.16.

FIGURE 6.16 Turn on the Messages tool using the Settings app.

You need to sign in with your Apple ID on the right side by entering the email address you use as your Apple ID and the password and then clicking the Sign In button.

> TIP: **Your Apple ID**
> Most iPad users create their Apple ID when they first install iTunes. If you haven't created an account yet, tap the Create New Account button shown in Figure 6.16 and follow the instructions. An Apple ID is required to use the Messaging feature.

After your Apple ID is verified, you are presented with a new screen like the one shown in Figure 6.17.

You can use the same email address used in your Apple ID or enter a new one. After entering an email address to use with the Messaging app, click the Next button.

Enter email address

FIGURE 6.17   Provide an email address to use for messaging.

TIP: **Confirm the Messages Email Address You Provided**
Apple sends an email message to the email you provide. Inside that email is a link that you must click to verify the validity of your Apple ID. You need to enter the Apple ID and password to prove your identity and confirm that the email address you provided for use with the Messages app is an address that you have access to.

The Messages app is now enabled and you see a list of other options related to using the Messages app (see Figure 6.18). I suggest leaving them set to their default selections, but feel free to experiment with them to discover how they work (or consult the iPad User's Guide for more details).

FIGURE 6.18   The Messages app is enabled and ready to use.

Notice in Figure 6.18 that you can turn the Messages app on and off by toggling the iMessage button. You might want to do this if you find yourself in a situation (such as hastily trying to finish writing a chapter for your editor) where pop-up messaging alerts (from a friend asking "Whatcha doin?") can slow you down and interrupt your train of thought (thanks, Jeff). Temporarily turning off the ability to send and receive instant messages can really help you get some work done.

Okay, now that you've turned on the Messages app, let's take a look at how you use it. Return to the Home screen and tap the Messages app to open it. A screen like the one shown in Figure 6.19 displays.

Type the email address of the other person who is running the Messages app or select them from the Contacts app by clicking the + sign indicated in Figure 6.19.

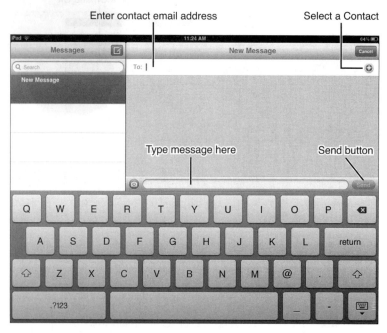

FIGURE 6.19   A blank instant messaging screen.

TIP: **Messages Isn't for Everyone**
Until Apple changes things, the Messages app only works for those users who have it enabled on an iPhone, an iPod Touch, or an iPad.

After you enter the name of the person in the To: field, type your message in the short text field indicated in Figure 6.20. Your typing scrolls to the right and the wraps to a new line, but the goal with instant messaging is to try to keep your individual messages short. Click the Send button when you want to send the message to your contact.

After your contact receives your message, he or she can type a response and then click his or her own Send button. Figure 6.21 shows a back and forth conversation between me and my extremely intelligent and super-sweet editor, Laura.

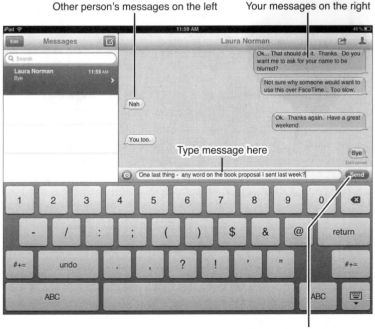

FIGURE 6.20   Beginning a conversation with a contact.

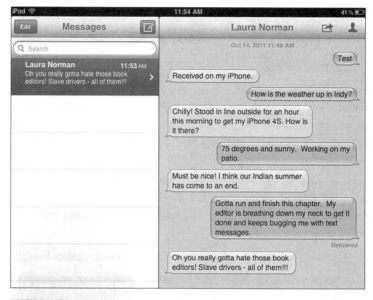

FIGURE 6.21   An intelligent conversation begins.

After you finish an instant messaging session with your contact, a copy of the conversation (well, the text of that conversation) is saved. You can access the transcript in the left-side Messages List (refer to Figure 6.21). If you want to delete a conversation when it's over, tap a conversation to open it and then tap the Edit button. Tap the – (minus) button that appears to the left of the conversation and then click the Delete button to delete that instant messaging session.

Summary

We covered a lot in this lesson, but the Notes, Contacts, and Messages apps are easy to use. You can now create, edit, and delete notes and contacts. You also learned to use the Messages app to have a back-and-forth conversation with a contact.

LESSON 7

Using the App Store

In this lesson, you learn to use the App Store to search and download both free apps and paid apps.

The App Store

The iPad comes with 20 great pre-installed apps when you buy the tablet, but, just as with a computer, you have the ability to install many more applications on your iPad. You can download productivity apps, games, digital books, educational apps, and much more. And just when you think you've seen it all, a new app is released that is difficult to categorize.

Your gateway to all these new apps is called the App Store. To access it you use an app that's already installed on your iPad. The easiest way to understand this app is to simply open it and try it out. So tap the app icon you see in Figure 7.1 and let's take the App Store for a spin.

FIGURE 7.1   The App Store app icon.

NOTE: **The App Store Takes Time to Learn**
There is no possible way to cover every little feature that the App Store offers. Instead, I show you the most basic uses for it: downloading and installing an app, updating your apps, and using the search feature. You need to consult the iPad User's Guide for additional information related to using the App Store.

When you open the App Store app for the first time, you might be a bit overwhelmed by what you see. It reminds me of the view from Times Square in New York City where you're flooded with imagery and text. (Fortunately, the App Store is quiet with no background sounds or sales pitches.)

I discuss the App Store using Horizontal View so the screen is less crowded, which makes it easier to identify things. Figure 7.2, for example, shows an animated box at the top that cycles through new and interesting apps that Apple thinks you might be interested in. Below that box you see smaller advertisements for six new apps along with their price and a rating (from 1 to 5 stars). You can tap the indicated arrow to view the next six apps on page 2, followed by pages 3 and 4.

FIGURE 7.2   The App Store is all about presenting apps to you.

Use your finger to scroll down the page and the next two sections you see are shown in Figure 7.3. These include buttons that take you to specific categories (such as Games or Education) or certain paid advertisers (such as *The New Yorker* magazine). Below these buttons are the Staff Favorites, another four pages (indicated by the four small dots) with six apps on each page.

Category buttons   Paid Advertisers

FIGURE 7.3   View categories or Staff Favorites.

I return to the Staff Favorites section in a moment, but let's finish up our tour of the App Store by scrolling down just a bit more to see the last few options available.

Figure 7.4 shows a set of Quick Links that can help you get some apps quickly on your iPad. Tapping the iPad Apps Starter Kit, for example, presents you with a mixture of free and paid apps that Apple feels every iPad owner should consider putting on her tablet. You can also see the iPad Games Starter Kit, a collection of games that, again, Apple thinks every iPad gamer should experience. You can also find links to the iPad Hall of Fame, Apps and Games of the Week, and a link to the iWork collection of productivity apps sold by Apple.

Quick Links

Welcome James!

| iPad Apps Starter Kit | iPad Games Starter Kit | iPad Hall of Fame |
| Previous Apps of the Week | Previous Games of the Week | iWork |

| Apple ID: jim@bluerocketwriting.com | Redeem | Support |

iTunes Store Terms and Conditions...

FIGURE 7.4   Quick Links and additional App Store buttons.

Below the Quick Links section is your Apple ID, a Redeem button, and a Support button. (More on these later in the lesson.)

Finally, at the very bottom of the App Store is a toolbar with six buttons as shown in Figure 7.5.

FIGURE 7.5   The App Store toolbar offers six options.

The Featured button is what you currently see. It's often considered the App Store's homepage. Tapping the Top Charts button, presents you with a list of the best-selling apps and the most popular free apps. The Categories button breaks down all the apps sold in the App Store to 20 categories (such as Lifestyle, Books, or Sports). Tap a category to view apps in that category. The Purchased button displays all apps that you've bought and offers you the chance to install them to your iPad. Simply tap the Purchased button and then tap the cloud icon next to any apps that appear to download them to your iPad.

The Genius button, when first tapped, requires you to turn on the feature. If you choose to enable it, information related to your browsing and buying habits is sent to Apple. The benefit to allowing this exchange of information is that the Genius tool provides app suggestions to you based on what it sees as your interests and needs from previous app installations.

Finally, use the Updates button to get updates (including bug fixes) to apps that you have installed on your iPad. I show you how the Updates feature works later in this lesson, but for now all you need to know is that if you see a small number (called a badge) in the upper-right corner of the Updates button (in Figure 7.5 there's a 1 badge) that number represents the number of apps you have on your iPad that have an existing update that you can apply. Again, I show you how this works shortly.

Okay, so now that you know the basics of what is what in the App Store, go grab a free app and install it. Return to Figure 7.3 and tap on the IMDb Movies & TV app (it's free to install). Anytime you tap the icon representing an app, you see a screen similar to the one in Figure 7.6. This is an app's information screen.

In addition to the price of the app (this one is free), you can read a description (click the More button to expand the Description field), read about the features in the latest version, use a swipe gesture to view screen captures of the app, and—if you scroll to the bottom of the page—read customer reviews and see an overall rating for the app (see Figure 7.7).

Price (or Free)   Click to read more

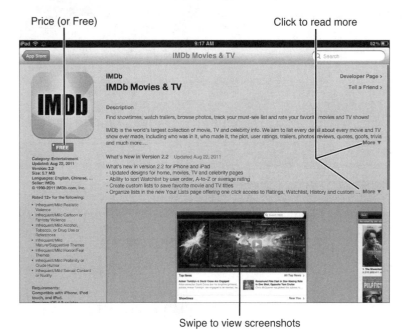

Swipe to view screenshots

FIGURE 7.6   An app's information screen offers more details about the app.

After reading some reviews, examining the screenshots, and determining from the description that you want to install the app, simply click the Free button (refer to Figure 7.6). The button turns into the Install App button shown in Figure 7.8.

After you tap the Install App button, you must provide your Apple ID password as shown in Figure 7.9.

After you enter your password, the App Store app closes and the app begins to install as shown in Figure 7.10.

Customer reviews   Rating 1-5 stars

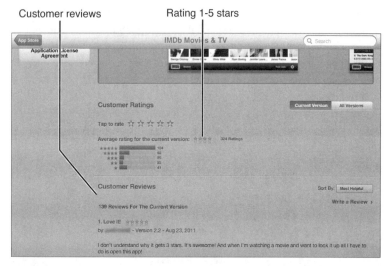

FIGURE 7.7   Read customer reviews and view the app's rating.

Click to begin installation

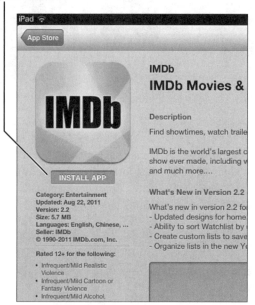

FIGURE 7.8   Choose to download the app by tapping the Free button, which turns into the Install App button.

FIGURE 7.9   Provide your Apple ID and password to begin the install.

Progress bar
for installation

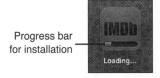

FIGURE 7.10   Your app is installed on a Home screen.

NOTE: **Turn on Automatic Downloads**
If you own an iPhone or other iPad and have apps that you've already purchased, you need to turn on the automatic downloads feature so these apps reinstall on your iPad 2. To do this, open the Settings app, tap on Store in the Settings List, and then on the right side of the screen tap the Apps button so the toggle button turns to the On position.

After the app installs, you can tap the app's icon to open it. Most apps have a Help feature or built-in instructions, so you need to consult the built-in documentation for each app to learn how it works.

I just showed you how to download a free app, but the process for buying an app is almost identical. The only difference is that instead of tapping the Free button on an app's information page, you need to tap the price button. Similarly, instead of the Install App button, you see a Buy App button like the one in Figure 7.11.

Tap to
buy app

FIGURE 7.11 Buy an app by tapping the app's price button, which turns into the Buy App button.

Tap the Buy App button and you once again have to provide your Apple ID password. To purchase apps, you also must provide a credit card number that is kept on file and charged when you make a purchase. You should have done this when you installed iTunes, but if you haven't yet done so, consult the iTunes help documentation for the steps to save a credit card on file.

After purchasing the app, it loads on your iPad and is ready to use when the installation progress bar (indicated by the blue bar—refer to Figure 7.10) finishes.

Updating an App

App developers, including Apple itself, frequently release updates to the apps they sell (or give away). When you purchase an app, you are typically provided with free updates to the app. I say typically because some developers do release trial versions of their apps in addition to full versions; often times both the free trial versions and the full versions get updates, but not always. You might find yourself forced to purchase a full version for a specific update or feature, so just know that updates sometimes are only available after you purchase a full version of an app.

I already showed you how the App Store app displays a badge on the Update button to indicate the number of apps that have an update available. But what if you're not running the App Store app? Well, in that instance, you need to keep an eye on the App Store app icon (see Figure 7.12). Even when the App Store app isn't open, you still find that the updates badge pops up in the upper-right corner of the App Store app icon to alert you to updates.

 Number of app
updates available

FIGURE 7.12   The App Store app icon alerts you to updates.

If an update is indicated, tap the App Store app to open it and then tap the Updates button on the bottom toolbar (refer to Figure 7.5). You can also tap the Updates button any time you want to force the App Store app to check for updates.

When updates are available, they are listed as shown in Figure 7.13.

Tap the Update button to the right of any app to immediately begin updating that app, or tap the Update All button near the top-right corner and update them all at once. Keep in mind that updating a large number of apps at once can often take more than a few minutes. You'll also be happy to know you can continue to work on your iPad—browse the internet, or maybe check email—while the updates install in the background.

Deleting an App

If you tire of an app you can remove it from your iPad temporarily or forever. When you purchase an app, it is always available for download again, so there's no need to worry about accidentally deleting an app and having to purchase it again. The only apps you cannot delete are the 20 pre-installed apps that come with your newly purchased iPad.

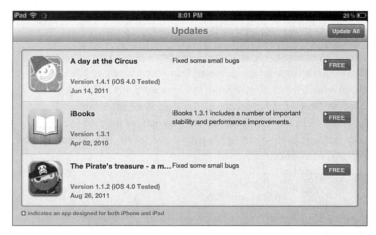

FIGURE 7.13   Apps with updates available are listed.

To delete an app, tap and hold your finger on any app until you see the app icons with circled x's in the upper-left corners. The icons should be wiggling (see Figure 7.14).

FIGURE 7.14   Preparing to delete an app.

Tap the X on the app (or apps) you want to remove and then tap the Delete button in the confirmation window (see Figure 7.15).

FIGURE 7.15   Confirm that you want to delete an app.

If you read the confirmation window carefully, you see the downside to deleting an app. When you remove an app, all data associated with that app is deleted as well.

Deleting all the data might not be a big deal to you, but then again, if you've been playing a game with 30 levels and you've only made your way up to Level 10, you lose your progress and have to start over if you ever choose to install that game app again. The same goes for other apps. The to-do list app, when deleted, also takes with it any reminders you have stored.

One exception that I can think of are the eBook readers such as the Kindle or Nook apps. Deleting them doesn't delete the digital books you've purchased through their services. If you delete and then reinstall the Kindle app, for example, you have access to download all your purchased eBooks again. There are likely other exceptions to other types of apps, but as a rule, be very careful when deleting apps and understand the risks of data loss.

Searching the App Store

You can download apps based on reviews you read in magazines or on blogs. In these instances, you know exactly what you're looking for and, after opening up the App Store app, you can simply type the name of the app in the Search bar indicated in Figure 7.16.

As you type, possible matches display in a drop-down box (refer to Figure 7.16). Tap one of the search results if you think it is a match. Alternatively, you can hit the Search button on the on-screen keyboard to get a complete list of matches as shown in Figure 7.17.

FIGURE 7.16   Use the Search bar to find exact app names.

FIGURE 7.17   Possible matches to the search are listed.

At this point, you can click an app's Free or price buttons to download and install it (if you see the one you want), or you can tap an app's icon to read more details on its information page.

It really helps to either have an app's full name or at least know its category. Without that kind of information, you are forced to do the needle-in-haystack search that can really take some time given that the App Store currently has more than 425,000 apps available. (Check out http://en.wikipedia.org/wiki/App_Store_(iOS) to see how many more apps might be available at the time you read this book.)

When searching for a specific app, I prefer to select a category first (tap the Categories button shown in Figure 7.5) and then use the search bar to try to narrow down my search using keywords. For example, the Astronomy category is shown in Figure 7.18.

FIGURE 7.18   Searching a category within the App Store app.

Any keywords you enter into the search bar while viewing a category return only the results found inside that category. As you can see in Figure 7.19, a search for "writing" while browsing the Education category returned some educational apps that teach writing skills.

FIGURE 7.19   Search results are applied within a category.

Notice also in Figure 7.19 that there are even more powerful search tools available along the top, including the ability to change the category, specify a minimum rating or price (free or paid), and more.

Redeeming an App Code

Someday you might receive an app code either as a gift from a friend or as a possible trial for an app that hasn't yet been released. (This sometimes happens when you register your software; developers love to test their new apps by offering them to existing customers.)

When you receive an app code, you need to open the App Store app and scroll to the bottom where you see the Redeem button (refer to Figure 7.4).

After you tap the Redeem button, you see a screen like the one in Figure 7.20.

FIGURE 7.20   The Redeem button lets you enter an app code.

Tap inside the Code text box and enter the code using the onscreen keyboard. Next, tap the Redeem button.

You have to sign in with your Apple ID, so provide that information when requested. After providing the Apple ID password, you see an alert like the one in Figure 7.21. You can enter another code or press the Home button and go check out your newly downloaded app.

FIGURE 7.21   Enter another code or go open your new app.

Creating Folders for Apps

The App Store is your one-stop-shop for finding and installing apps of interest to you. Whether you use your iPad for work, personal, or both, you'll likely find over time that your iPad begins to fill up with more and more apps. Pretty soon, you're spending a good amount of time just swiping between Home screens to find your app.

Fortunately, your iPad has a great way to organize your apps when they begin to get out of control. Folders enable you to group apps in any manner you like. I prefer to create folders with names such as My Games and Kids Games.

To create a folder, start with two apps that you want to join. In Figure 7.22, I want to combine the Doodle Buddy app and the Circus app into a folder titled Kids Stuff.

FIGURE 7.22   Combine apps to create a folder.

First, tap and hold one of the apps until it begins to dance on the screen. When the apps are dancing, drag one of the apps and drop it on top of the other app (see Figure 7.22). (For some odd reason, my iPad chooses to name the folder Productivity—strange!)

The two apps combine in a folder, which you can rename (see Figure 7.23).

Tap anywhere on the screen to return to the dancing apps. Drag and drop more apps into the new folder (see Figure 7.24) or tap the Home button to stop the wiggling apps. Create as many folders as you like using this method, but keep in mind that each folder holds a maximum of 20 apps.

FIGURE 7.23   Name the folder anything you like.

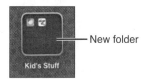
— New folder

FIGURE 7.24   A new folder is created.

When the apps and folders are wiggling, you can tap and hold a folder or app and drag it to the far left or right edge to move it to another home screen. I like to move all my folders to the last Home screen (the one farthest to the right using swipes) but you might choose to put all folders on the primary Home screen. Wherever you choose to put them, I highly encourage you to use folders to keep your iPad organized.

Summary

In this lesson you learned all about the App Store, including how to find, download, and install both free and paid apps. You learned how to apply updates to your installed apps and how to use folders to organize your growing collection of apps.

LESSON 8

Accessing and Using Books, Magazines, and Music

This lesson highlights various aspects of the iBooks app. You learn how to obtain books using iBooks and how to use the app to read a book, annotate, search, and more.

The iBooks App

Apple provides the iBooks app free to you, but you must download it from the App Store (although you don't have to use it—options exist such as the Kindle and Nook apps). Visit the App Store to search for, download, and install iBooks. (Refer to Lesson 7, "Using the App Store," if you need a refresher on how to find and download an app.) After installing iBooks, the icon appears on your iPad (see Figure 8.1).

FIGURE 8.1   The iBooks app installed on the iPad.

When you first open iBooks, you see an empty bookcase as shown in Figure 8.2.

Click to
visit iBooks ───
Store

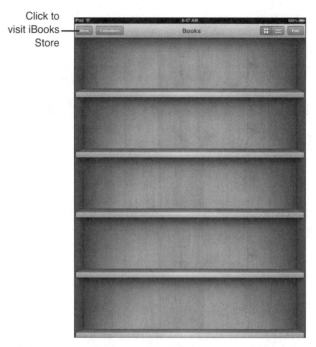

FIGURE 8.2   Your iPad's bookshelf is empty at first.

> NOTE: **Synchronizing Existing Book Purchases**
> If you've previously purchased books on another iPad, or maybe
> your iPhone or iPod Touch, you learn how to download them later in
> this lesson. Don't worry—you won't have to repurchase books
> through iBooks.

Buying and Downloading Books

Buying a book is simple; it works just like purchasing apps. You need an
Apple ID and a credit card on file. Tap the Store button indicated in Figure
8.2 and the iBooks Store opens as shown in Figure 8.3.

Like the App Store (refer to Lesson 7), some featured books cycle at the
top of the opening screen in iBooks; tapping one takes you to that book's
information screen.

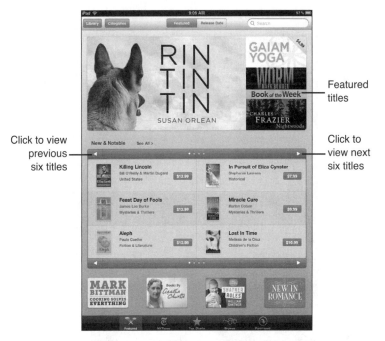

Click to view
previous
six titles

Featured
titles

Click to
view next
six titles

FIGURE 8.3   The iBooks Store works just like the App Store.

Below the featured books are the New & Notable books—four pages of six books each. Use the Previous and Next buttons to cycle through the list.

Scroll down a bit more and you see additional categories and buttons as shown in Figure 8.4.

Toward the bottom of the screen, you find a New category. In the example shown, you see New Mysteries & Thrillers, but this changes from time to time. To view all 24 newly released titles on one screen, tap the See All link. Or, simply use the Previous and Next buttons to view six books at a time.

Below the second category of books is a collection of links that changes now and then—in Figure 8.4 you see the Big Fall Releases link as well as Popular Pre-Orders and other links that the iBooks Store suggests, based on your previous selections.

Tap to view all featured titles

Special categories and collections

Redeem button

FIGURE 8.4   More options are available in the iBooks Store.

Finally, just as you can redeem gift codes with the App Store, you can also redeem codes for books using the Redeem button. The steps are the same as those described in Lesson 7 for the App Store.

To search for a book and make a purchase, you can use the Search bar indicated in Figure 8.5, or you could tap the Top Charts button (also indicated in Figure 8.5) to check out top sellers and top free books.

When you tap a title of interest, you go to that book's information page (see Figure 8.6).

The information page includes the price button (or a Free button) to tap if you want to buy a book (or download it in the case of free books). By scrolling down the page a bit, you can read a written description of the book as well as customer reviews.

Search bar

Click to view Top Charts

FIGURE 8.5   Top Charts gives me a list of the top sellers and freebies.

Other information available on the page includes the publisher's name, the page count, the category, and more. You can tap the Author's Page link to view a list of other books for sale by this author. Another feature available is Tell a Friend, which you can tap to send an email message with a link to the book to one of your friends.

For some books you can download a sample chapter or a fixed number of pages. Tap the Get Sample button indicated in Figure 8.6 to read a section of the book before you make a purchase decision.

If you choose to purchase a book, tap the price button. You need to provide your Apple ID and password before the book's download begins.

Tap to buy (or download if free)   Tap to download sample pages

FIGURE 8.6   An eBook's information page.

When you have purchased a book, it appears on the bookshelf as shown in Figure 8.7.

FIGURE 8.7   Your purchases appear on the bookshelf.

Reading a Book

A new banner indicates the newly downloaded book. Tap the cover of the book to open it and begin reading. The first time you open a book the copyright information page displays, as seen in Figure 8.8.

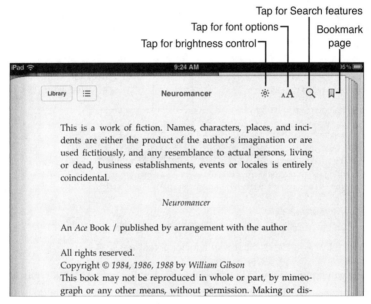

FIGURE 8.8 A book opened and ready to be read.

To turn a page, swipe it with your finger from the right to left (to read the next page) or left to right (to return to a previous page). As you swipe your finger, you see the page turn.

At the top of the screen, you can tap the Brightness button to adjust the brightness of the screen. Tap the Fonts button to adjust the size of the words on the screen as well as the color of the page (your options are Sepia and White). You can tap the magnifying glass to search the book for a keyword you enter with the on-screen keyboard, and you can tap the bookmark icon to save your spot in the book. To close the book, tap the Library button to return to the bookshelf or tap the Home button to exit the iBooks app.

There are several other useful features in the iBooks app. Below are just a few of the additional tools available.

Dictionary

When you read a book and you encounter a new word, you can tap and hold your finger on that word to get access to the small toolbar shown in Figure 8.9.

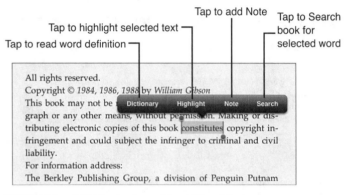

FIGURE 8.9   A hidden toolbar with additional features.

When you tap the Dictionary button indicated in Figure 8.9, a small window appears that gives the definition of the selected word. Other options in this toolbar enable you to highlight a word or even an entire sentence; leave a note similar to writing in the margins of a real book; and search for other instances of the selected word.

Navigation

You might occasionally need to flip back and forth between chapters or sections of a book. The iBooks app makes this easy to do with two options. The first option uses the small box icon indicated in Figure 8.10.

Tap and hold your finger on the box indicated in Figure 8.10 and then drag your finger to the left or right. Dragging your finger to the left moves you closer to the beginning of the book, indicated by the page counter in Figure 8.11. Dragging your finger to the right moves you further to the end of the book.

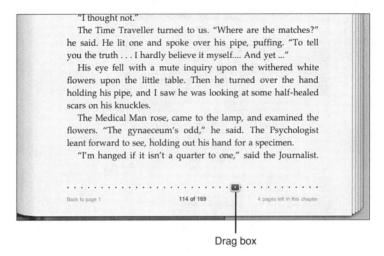

"I thought not."

The Time Traveller turned to us. "Where are the matches?" he said. He lit one and spoke over his pipe, puffing. "To tell you the truth . . . I hardly believe it myself.... And yet ..."

His eye fell with a mute inquiry upon the withered white flowers upon the little table. Then he turned over the hand holding his pipe, and I saw he was looking at some half-healed scars on his knuckles.

The Medical Man rose, came to the lamp, and examined the flowers. "The gynaeceum's odd," he said. The Psychologist leant forward to see, holding out his hand for a specimen.

"I'm hanged if it isn't a quarter to one," said the Journalist.

Back to page 1   **114 of 169**   4 pages left in this chapter

Drag box

FIGURE 8.10   The drag box icon allows you to move forward and back through a book.

This feature is a bit like shooting in the dark, as you only get the chapter title (or number) and the page number to reference. It's useful for going back to a very specific page number, but not much use if you don't know the page number you want. In most cases, you'd probably prefer to jump directly to the beginning of a chapter. To do this, use the Table of Contents button indicated in Figure 8.11. Tap that button to go to the Table of Contents as shown in Figure 8.12.

When you view the Table of Contents, tap on a specific chapter to jump directly to the start of that chapter. Keep in mind that if the Table of Contents is long, you must swipe up on the touchscreen to view the remaining chapter listings that are hidden below.

Adding Notes and Commentary

If you like to write in the margins of your print books, you may find it a bit difficult with digital versions of books. Fortunately the iBooks app does allow you to add in your own notes and commentary using the on-screen keyboard.

Table of
Contents
button

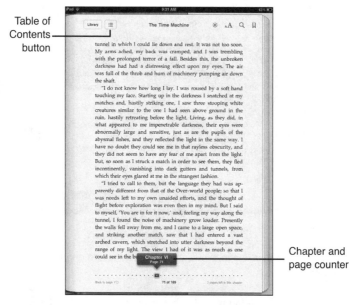

Chapter and
page counter

FIGURE 8.11   Use the drag box and counter to move to a new page.

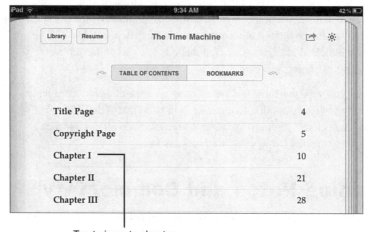

Tap to jump to chapter

FIGURE 8.12   Use the Table of Contents button to find specific chapters.

Find a place where you wish to add a note and then tap your finger on a word (preferably at the beginning of a sentence or paragraph). A small menu appears like the one in Figure 8.13.

Tap the Note option on the menu and a note card appears on screen along with the on-screen keyboard. Type your note as shown in Figure 8.14.

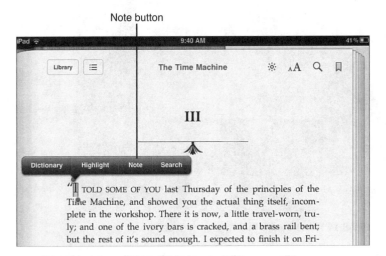

FIGURE 8.13   Tap in the book where you wish to add a note.

Tap anywhere outside of the note to close it down and you see a small sticky-note added to the margin, with the date the note was added. Additionally, the word you tapped to create the note is highlighted as shown in Figure 8.15. Tap the note to re-open it for reading or editing purposes. Tap the highlighted word to delete the note.

Finally, if you want to view all your notes added to a digital book, first tap the Table of Contents button as previously discussed. Then, tap the Bookmarks button indicated in Figure 8.16 to see your notes listed along with page number, date, and a small snippet of the original book's text.

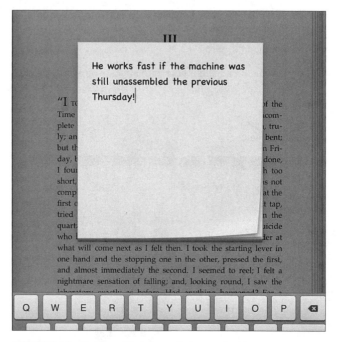

FIGURE 8.14   Add a note to a page in your book.

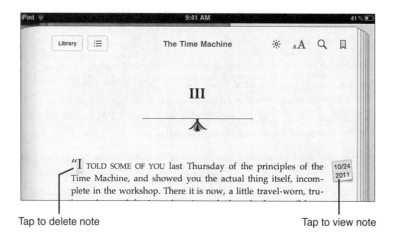

Tap to delete note

Tap to view note

FIGURE 8.15   Your notes are added to the margins.

Tap to view notes

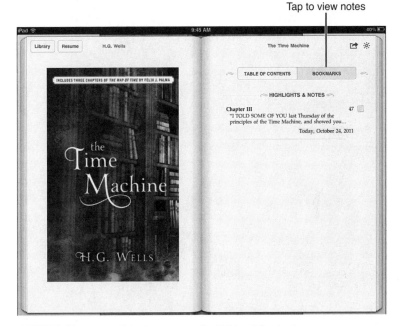

FIGURE 8.16 View all your notes on the Table of Contents page.

Summary

In this lesson you learned all about using your iPad as a personal reader with the iBooks app. You learned to search for books, make purchases, read downloaded books, and use additional features such as the built-in Dictionary, the Table of Contents navigation tool, and more.

LESSON 9

Photos and FaceTime

The iPad 2 comes with a built-in digital camera and a webcam, perfect tools for taking photos, shooting some video, and having a face-to-face chat with a friend or family member. In this lesson you learn all about the Camera app and the FaceTime app.

The Camera App

The iPad 2's digital camera is on the backside of the tablet. (Unfortunately, the original iPad did not come with a camera or webcam, so you can skip this lesson or continue to read if you want to upgrade to an iPad 2.) The camera takes photos at just under 1 megapixel (0.92 according to some websites), so you can't shoot any magazine covers with it just yet. However, the camera does enable you to shoot video at 720p (HD), which is a nice touch.

To take photos or shoot video, you use the Camera app. Go ahead and tap the icon (see Figure 9.1) to launch the app.

FIGURE 9.1   The Camera app icon on your iPad.

When you open the Camera app, you see a simple screen like the one in Figure 9.2.

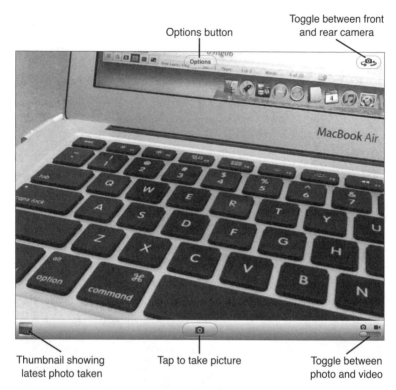

Options button

Toggle between front
and rear camera

MacBook Air

Thumbnail showing
latest photo taken

Tap to take picture

Toggle between
photo and video

FIGURE 9.2   The Camera opens and is ready to take a photo.

CAUTION: **Embedding Your Location in Photos**

The first time you open the Camera app you are asked whether you
want to allow photos to have the location (where the photo was
taken) embedded in the digital file. Your choices are don't allow it
or allow it. If you take a nice photo of your new car sitting in the
garage and post that photo on the internet for the world to see,
you could be telling a car thief the vehicle's exact location.
Fortunately you can turn this feature off in the Settings app under
the Location Services option in the Settings List. Choose Location
Services and toggle the Camera On or Off on the right side of the
screen.

Remember, the iPad rotates, so the Camera app takes photos or videos in
Horizontal View or Vertical View. For the remainder of this lesson I use

Horizontal View, but the buttons and functionality work identically when you use Vertical View.

Let's start at the bottom of the screen. Here you find a small toggle button (refer to Figure 9.2) that switches the Camera app between shooting photos and shooting video.

The Camera app displays a small icon of a camera on the shutter button when it is set to take a photo. Hold the iPad up, frame your subject, and then tap the shutter button to take the picture. You see an animation on the screen like the shutter on a real camera closing and then opening to let you know the photo has been captured.

After you take a photo, a small thumbnail of the photo displays in the lower-left corner (refer to Figure 9.2).

Tap the thumbnail of the photo you just took and it opens as shown in Figure 9.3.

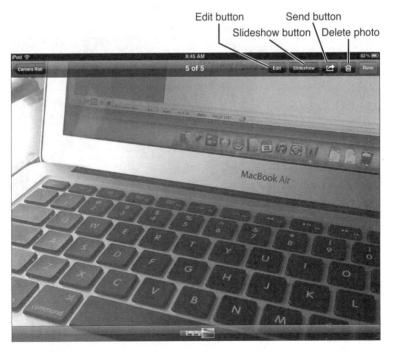

FIGURE 9.3   Viewing the most recent photo you took.

Before returning to the Camera app, let's take a look at the options available to you while you view your most recent photo.

Tap the Edit button (refer to Figure 9.3) to perform special actions, such as rotating the image, cropping the photo, or removing red-eye.

Tap the Slideshow button to immediately launch a slideshow of all the photos stored in the Gallery (see Lesson 11, "Using the Photos App").

Tap the Send button to email the photo, use it as the iPad's wallpaper, print it out, and a few other options covered in Lesson 11.

Tap the trashcan icon to delete the photo.

Swipe the screen (left or right) to flip through all the digital images stored on your iPad.

Return to the Camera app by tapping the Done button. Figure 9.4 shows the screen you see when you choose the Options button (visible at the top

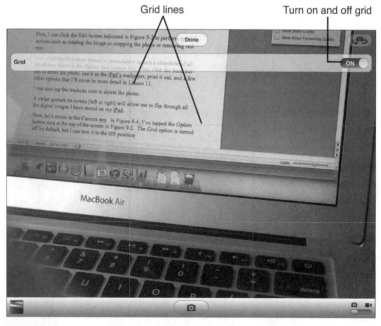

FIGURE 9.4   Turning the 3X3 grid on using the Options feature.

of the screen in Figure 9.2). The Grid option turns off by default, but when you turn it to the On position, a 3X3 grid overlays the screen.

You don't have to be a professional photographer to learn about the picture-taking tip called the Rule of Thirds. You can read more about it at http://en.wikipedia.org/wiki/Rule_of_thirds. In a nutshell, the tip says that photos are more engaging when the subject of the photo is not centered but instead is moved more to the left third or right third of the screen (or the top third or bottom third, depending on the nature of the photo).

The grid feature is all about helping you use the Rule of Thirds, but feel free to leave it turned off if you don't like it.

In the top-right corner of the Camera app (refer to Figure 9.2) another toggle button enables you to switch back and forth between the digital camera on the back of the iPad and the webcam on the front. You can use this, for example, to take photos or shoot video of yourself. Most of the time, however, you want to use the iPad's screen and the rear-facing camera to take photos and videos.

To shoot video, tap the toggle button indicated in Figure 9.2 so that the rear-facing camera is set to take video. Notice that the camera icon on the shutter button disappears and a red (Record) dot replaces it, as seen in Figure 9.5.

Record button

FIGURE 9.5   The Camera app is set to record video.

The video-recording function works the same way as the picture-taking function; hold the iPad so that what you want to record displays on the touchscreen and then tap the Record button to begin recording video. If the volume is turned up, you hear a quiet beep to indicate you are recording.

To see how much video you have so far, look at the timer in the upper-right corner as shown in Figure 9.6.

Length of current video

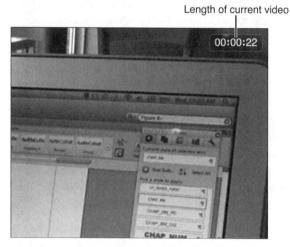

00:00:22

FIGURE 9.6   Twenty-two seconds of video so far.

Tap the Record button again to stop the video recording. You can then tap the thumbnail in the lower-left corner of the screen to view the video you just shot.

Lesson 11 covers the Photos app, where you learn to view and edit your digital photos and view videos. Before we leave the Camera app, let's look at how to trim the videos that you shoot.

Unfortunately, the editing capabilities provided by the Camera app are extremely limited. For this reason, I encourage you to search the App Store if you want to find more advanced editing features for videos. You can always transfer your videos from the iPad to a computer that runs video-editing software, but that's an unnecessary step if you choose to download and install a video-editing app made especially for the iPad. One of the most popular right now is actually Apple's own iMovie (see Figure 9.7), and its $4.99 price is great for a powerful video-editing app designed specifically for the iPad 2.

FIGURE 9.7 iMovie provides video-editing features not found in the Camera app.

Although the Camera app has very few video-editing capabilities to speak of, it does enable you to trim your videos. This can be a useful feature to reduce the size and length of videos.

After shooting a video, tap the thumbnail to open the video (see Figure 9.8).

To watch the video, tap the Play button located in the center of the touch-screen and the entire video plays (with sound if the volume is turned up).

If you decide to trim the video, tap anywhere on the video except on the Play button and a menu bar displays as shown in Figure 9.9.

Touch and drag down slightly at the start of the video frame box indicated in Figure 9.9. If you do this correctly, a yellow box appears around all of the frames of your video (see Figure 9.10).

Next, drag the left-most portion of the trim window to the right or the right-most portion of the trim window to the left to shorten the video.

Play button

FIGURE 9.8 You can view or edit an opened video.

Video frame box

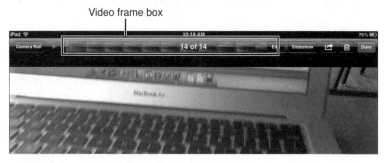

FIGURE 9.9 Use the toolbar to trim a video.

When you save the shortened version by tapping the Trim button, anything outside of the trim window is deleted.

The example in Figure 9.11 shows that just 5 seconds (of about 12) of video is selected to be saved.

Frames selected   Trim
                                   button

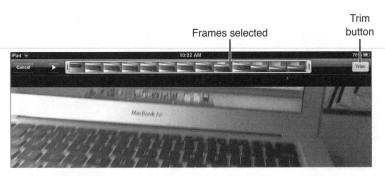

FIGURE 9.10   Select the collection of video frames to be trimmed.

Trimmed video

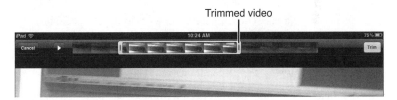

FIGURE 9.11   Tap the Trim button to make the cuts to your video.

When you tap the Trim button, you can choose to trim the original video or to save the edits as a new video clip. The first choice deletes video permanently, so there's no going back. The second option enables you to save the original video should you find that your trimming cut away something you really wanted to save. After you make your selection, the video editing finishes, and you can access and view your video using the Gallery app discussed in Lesson 11.

Face-to-Face Chats with FaceTime

If you've never used a webcam to have a video chat with a friend or family member, you're in for a treat. Your iPad comes with a front-mounted webcam and the FaceTime app that enables you to see and talk with others who run the FaceTime app on their Apple computers, iPhones, iPod Touches, or iPads.

Figure 9.12 shows the FaceTime app icon. Go ahead and tap it to open and run FaceTime.

FIGURE 9.12   The FaceTime app icon used for video chats.

Communicating via FaceTime requires both users to run the FaceTime app; fortunately the app is available for iPhone, iPad, and Mac users, so odds are that you have a few folks in your contact database who can let you try out FaceTime.

The first thing you want to do is determine whether any of your existing contacts have registered an email address for use with FaceTime. All contacts who appear down the right-side list as shown in Figure 9.13 use FaceTime with an email address that you have associated with their contact information.

FIGURE 9.13   FaceTime contacts appear in the All Contacts list.

If you want to connect with someone who has FaceTime on a device but has not yet used it, that person needs to open FaceTime and provide an email address before you attempt to make a call. Many people have multiple email addresses, so if a contact tells you she configured FaceTime with an email address but her name still doesn't show up in the All Contacts list, this likely means you need to add that person's FaceTime email address to her contact information. Use the Contacts app to add in this new email address and then return to FaceTime. That person's name now appears in the list.

If this is a completely new contact, you can tap the + button indicated in Figure 9.13 to create a new contact within FaceTime. Just be sure to add the email address that has associated with FaceTime.

When you have a contact's name in the All Contacts list, you can make a call. Tap that person's name to see a screen like the one in Figure 9.14, listing that person's email addresses.

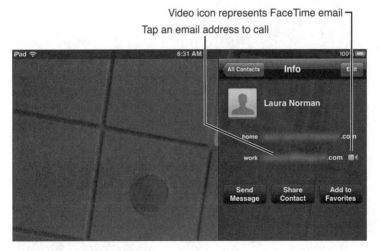

FIGURE 9.14   A Contact's email address information.

Tap the email address that corresponds to the one that your contact chose to use with FaceTime. You know which one it is because it has a small video icon next to it (refer to Figure 9.14).

After you tap the email address, FaceTime attempts to contact that person as shown in Figure 9.15.

Waiting for caller to pick up

FIGURE 9.15   FaceTime attempts a video call.

You know it's a success when you see your contact's bright, happy face on the screen along with a smaller box showing your own face. Figure 9.16

FIGURE 9.16   A FaceTime call between author and editor.

shows a FaceTime call in Horizontal View, but your iPad easily rotates to use FaceTime in Vertical View.

In Figure 9.16, you see a video chat between my editor, Laura, and me. She says I'm doing a great job on the book and wants to pay me more for future books. Or something like that.

At the bottom of the figure is the FaceTime toolbar. The Mute button does exactly what it says—it mutes the microphone until I tap it again to turn the sound back on.

The End button ends the FaceTime call, and the Swap button switches back and forth from the webcam (mounted on the front of the iPad and facing you if you look at the iPad's touchscreen) and the digital camera on back. This is a nice feature when you want to show your wife (who's at the office) the nice crayon drawing your two year old just did on the living room wall and see her facial expression at the same time, for instance. Simply point the iPad's digital camera at the artwork, tap the Swap button, and she sees what you point your iPad at while you view the screen to see her reaction.

TIP: **Move Your Own Image Around the Screen**
While using FaceTime, you can drag and drop the small box containing your own image to any of the four corners of the iPad screen. This might be useful to you if there's something in particular on the larger image (from the other person's webcam or camera) that is currently obscured by the small box containing your image.

Summary

In this lesson you learned how to use the camera on your iPad to take photos and the iPad's webcam to have a video chat using the FaceTime app.

Listening to Music

In this lesson, you learn how to use the Music App to purchase, download, and listen to music from iTunes. You also learn how to listen to music that you purchase from other sources or obtain from your CD collection.

The Music App

The most common method for listening to music on your iPad is to purchase and download it from iTunes. Entire books have been written on iTunes, and I don't have the space to cover the application, so instead, let me point you to *Sams Teach Yourself iTunes in 10 Minutes* for more details.

Most people install a copy of iTunes on a home computer or laptop, but you can also purchase music on your iPad without having to connect your iPad to a computer.

To get started, tap the Music icon (typically located on the Dock) as shown in Figure 10.1. (Prior to iOS 5, this icon was named iPod after Apple's digital music player of the same name.)

FIGURE 10.1 The Music app icon on your iPad.

When Music opens, you see a screen like the one shown in Figure 10.2.

Tap to play song

Volume control

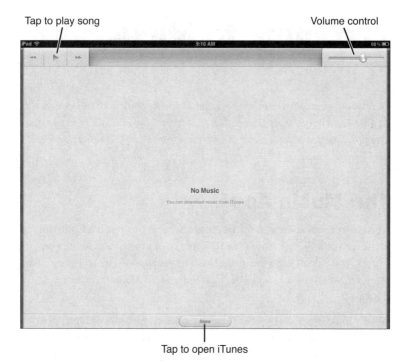

Tap to open iTunes

FIGURE 10.2	The Music app is empty to begin with.

Purchasing a Song

For now, let's assume that you don't already have any purchased music from iTunes. Later you learn how to import all of your purchased music easily.

The steps to find and purchase songs or albums are the same whether you already have purchased music from iTunes or not, so start by tapping the Store button indicated in Figure 10.2. This opens the iTunes app (also found on the home screen) as shown in Figure 10.3.

If you read the earlier lessons on the App Store and the iBooks Store, then this interface should be quite familiar. At the top you find featured artists, albums, and even movies.

FIGURE 10.3 The iTunes Store is open and ready for business.

Further down you see the New & Noteworthy suggestions that list current popular items. Each has a price button so you can purchase the item right from this page.

As you continue to scroll down you see a link for Free Music at the bottom, along with the Redeem button (for redeeming iTunes gift cards) and other links, such as Pre-Orders, which you can use for media that's not yet released (see Figure 10.4).

iTunes sells more than music. You can purchase movies, TV shows, audiobooks, and even textbooks! Fortunately Apple doesn't mix all this up into one area of the iTunes app. At the very bottom of the app is a toolbar like the one in Figure 10.5. Tap any category, such as Music, Movies, or Audiobooks, to immediately filter the content and only show items for sale in the selected category.

You can experiment with all of the various categories later; but for now, let's learn how to find a song, buy it, and start listening. The process is the same whether you buy a song, a book, a movie, or a TV show.

Start by searching for an artist. If you know what you're looking for, you can easily search for an artist or a song title. Figure 10.6, for example, shows a search for The Beatles.

Tap to redeem gift cards

FIGURE 10.4   Redeem gift cards, get free music, and more.

FIGURE 10.5   Select a category using the iTunes toolbar.

FIGURE 10.6   Searching for a tune from The Beatles.

As you type the text into the search bar iTunes tries to guess what you want by offering possible items in the drop-down list. Suppose you want to take a look at The Beatles music from 1967 to 1970. Tap that option to view a screen like the one shown in Figure 10.7. Notice that the screen is broken into sections—Albums and Songs.

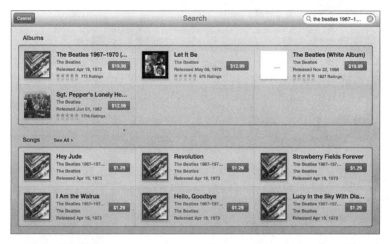

FIGURE 10.7   Use the search feature to find a particular song.

If you want to purchase an entire album, simply click on the price button to the right of the album's name and cover image.

TIP: **Getting the Best Bargain**

Individual songs purchased from iTunes run anywhere from $0.99 to $1.29, but if you purchase an entire album the cost per song often drops to below $0.89 per song, especially when the album contains more than 10 songs on it. For example, The Beatles entire 1967–1970 collection is listed at $19.99 and comes with 28 songs for an average price of $0.71 per song. If you think you might want a handful of songs from a single album, do the math and determine if it is cheaper to buy the entire album rather than buying only five or six individual songs from it.

In this example you see that the song "Revolution" costs $1.29. If you want to listen to 30 seconds of the song before purchasing, simply tap the song's image and a screen like the one in Figure 10.8 displays. The selected song is at the top of the list.

Selected song at top   Price button

FIGURE 10.8   Listen to a song before purchasing.

Tap the name of the song and it begins playing. A small timer displays to the left of the song's name (see Figure 10.9).

If you decide you want the song, tap the price button. It changes to another button labeled Buy Song. Tap that button and be ready to provide your Apple ID password. After you enter the password, the song begins to download. You can view the progress when you tap the Downloads button on the toolbar at the bottom of the screen and watch the download as it progresses (see Figure 10.10).

After the song downloads, you can click the Library button in the upper-left corner (indicated in Figure 10.10) to return to the Music app as shown in Figure 10.11.

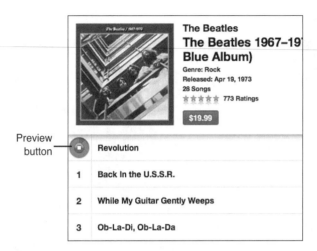

Preview button

FIGURE 10.9   Listen to the preview or tap the icon to stop it.

Library button   Download progress bar

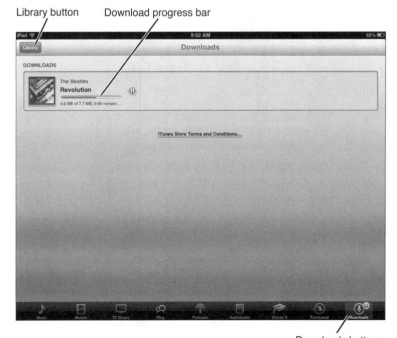

Downloads button

FIGURE 10.10   Downloading your song and viewing the progress.

Song download complete

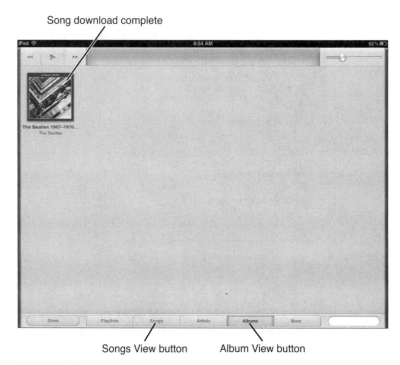

Songs View button   Album View button

FIGURE 10.11   The Music app shows the recent purchase.

Notice in Figure 10.11 that the buttons along the bottom of the screen indicate when you're in Album View. You can tap the Songs button to see all your music organized alphabetically by song title rather than grouped by album. Likewise, you can tap the Artists button and view all the songs grouped by artist name.

Figure 10.12 shows a song listed using the Songs button.

List of songs

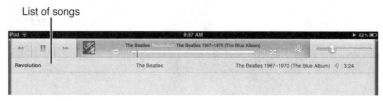

FIGURE 10.12   Viewing music using the Songs button.

Can you take a guess how to play a song? If you guessed that you simply
tap the name of the song, you're right. Figure 10.13 shows that
"Revolution" by The Beatles is now playing.

Pause button   Progress of song play

Store button

FIGURE 10.13   Listening to your new purchase.

Populating the Music app

Now, let's discuss how to populate the Music app with previously purchased music. Tap the Store button in the lower-left corner of Figure 10.13
(or open the iTunes app from the home screen). You may have already
noticed it, but take a look at the Purchased button on the toolbar indicated
in Figure 10.14. If you've purchased music from iTunes in the past, go
ahead and tap it.

Purchased button

FIGURE 10.14   The Purchased button lists all your purchased music.

A screen opens like the one shown in Figure 10.15.

All Songs button   Artist View   Not On This iPad button   Album View

FIGURE 10.15   Your previously purchased music is listed.

First, tap the Not On This iPad button indicated in Figure 10.15. This enables you to view the songs not currently saved on your iPad. You see a list on the left side of the screen that breaks your songs down by artist name. Tap the Albums button if you want to view the list by album name.

Tap an artist name (see Figure 10.16) to see a list of all the songs from that artist that you purchased from iTunes in the past. You can also tap the All Songs button to view the entire list of purchased songs.

Tap to download purchased song

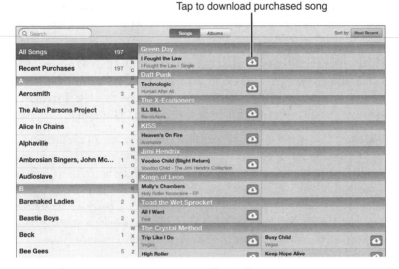

FIGURE 10.16 Viewing all songs in my iTunes library.

To select a song to download on your iPad, tap the iCloud button to the right of a song's name as indicated in Figure 10.16. You need to provide your Apple ID password to download the song.

Unfortunately, there does not appear to be a way to download all your purchased music at once, so you must tap the iCloud button for each and every song you want to pull down to your iPad.

Listening to Music from Other Sources

Before we leave this lesson, let's discuss a couple of other methods for listening to music with your iPad. This is a quick overview, so you might need to do a Google search if you require more details.

If you have a large CD collection like I do, it will please you to know that you can rip these CDs and store the digital song files on your iPad. You need to install the latest version of iTunes on a computer with a CD/DVD drive capable of playing the music CD.

First, open iTunes and insert a CD. By default, iTunes automatically converts the CD to digital files for use with iTunes, but you can change this in the File menu under Preferences.

iTunes automatically rips (copies) the music files from the CD to your iTunes library. When it is finished, eject the CD and insert a new one to start the process again. (Be warned—this process takes a while. I spent an entire day out of my weekend to rip a few hundred CDs I own.)

You should know that music you purchase from Amazon.com in the form of downloaded mp3 files can be easily downloaded to your iPad – read an Apple Support document that tells you how by visiting http://bit.ly/ 4to08B. However, Amazon.com also stores your purchased music in something it calls the Amazon Cloud Player. The songs you purchase are stored there indefinitely. You can access the Amazon.com website with Safari to play them. For more information, visit www.amazon.com and tap the Amazon Cloud Player button indicated in Figure 10.17.

Access the Amazon Cloud Player and tap the checkboxes for the songs you want to play. Then, click the Play button shown in Figure 10.18.

FIGURE 10.17   Amazon.com's Cloud Player is an online music player.

Check to select songs

Play button

FIGURE 10.18 Selecting songs in Amazon Cloud Player.

Finally, you might want to download the free Pandora app from the App Store. With an internet connection you can create virtual radio stations based on your interests. Search for artists or music styles you enjoy and watch Pandora queue up an endless list of songs from that artist and other similar-sounding bands.

Figure 10.19 shows the Pandora app. You can create radio stations based on your favorite bands. Tap the QuickMix button, indicated in Figure 10.19, and Pandora randomly jumps from band to band, playing a mix of songs from the bands you enjoy as well as new songs from bands that Pandora believes you'll enjoy based on your listening interests.

QuickMix button   Station list

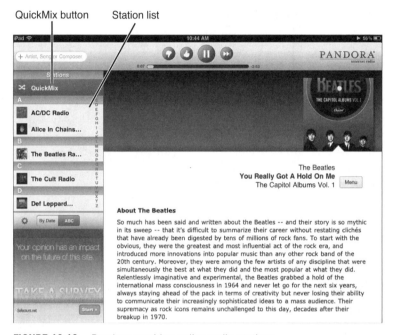

FIGURE 10.19   Pandora provides online radio stations.

Movies, TV, Books, and More

In addition to purchasing music with iTunes and listening to it with the Music app, the iTunes store sells movies, TV shows, audiobooks, and a few other things.

You can buy or rent movies (usually $4.99 for a 24-hour viewing period). TV shows are only available for purchase, not rent, but you have the option to purchase individual episodes similar to buying individual songs from an album.

You use the Videos app (see Lesson 12, "Working with Video and YouTube") to watch movies and TV shows. You play podcasts and audiobooks that you purchase with the Music app you've learned about in this lesson.

The Music app and the iTunes app have many more features that aren't covered in this lesson, so be sure to open them and poke around a bit or open up the iPad User Guide (inside the Safari app's Bookmarks menu) to learn more.

Summary

In this lesson you learned how to search for, purchase, download, and listen to music with the iTunes app and the Music app. You also learned about iTunes movie and TV show offerings and more. Finally, you learned about the Amazon Cloud Player, ripping music CDs, and the Pandora app.

Using the Photos App

In this lesson, you learn how to view, edit, and share your digital pictures and videos with the Photos app.

The Photos App

In Lesson 9, "Photos and FaceTime," you learned all about taking photos and videos using the Camera app. In this lesson you learn about the Photos app that enables you to view, edit, and share your photos and videos as well as a few additional options.

Figure 11.1 shows the Photos app icon. Go ahead and tap it to launch the app.

FIGURE 11.1   The Photos app icon on your iPad.

When the Photos app opens, you might see a screen similar to the one in Figure 11.2. If you have taken any photos or videos with the Camera app or if you've downloaded any images while you browse the web then you should see this screen. (If you don't already have photos, it would be helpful to open the Camera app and shoot a few images so you have something to work with as you read through this lesson.)

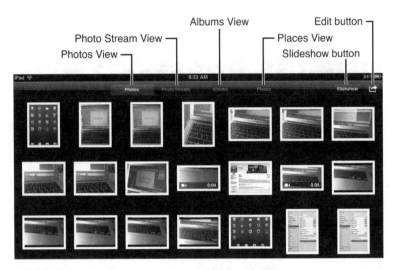

FIGURE 11.2   The Photos app stores images and video.

Along the top of the screen you see four buttons—Photos, Photo Stream, Albums, and Places. (The Slideshow button and the Action button are discussed a bit later in this lesson.)

The Photos Button

Let's start with the Photos button indicated in Figure 11.2. After you tap the Photos button, you see your images and videos displayed as thumbnails. Use a swipe gesture up and down to scroll so you can view thumbnails that are currently off-screen.

Video thumbnails are distinguished from photo thumbnails by a small video camera icon in the lower-left corner of the thumbnail.

Tap a photo image to see the thumbnail expand to fill the screen with the full image as shown in Figure 11.3.

After you open an image, the toolbar at the top of the screen indicated in Figure 11.3 disappears if you haven't touched the image for a few seconds. Simply tap anywhere on the screen again and the toolbar reappears. You can toggle the toolbar on and off at any time by tapping the image.

Toolbar   Edit button

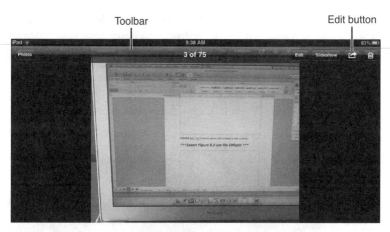

FIGURE 11.3   Tapping a thumbnail to view the enlarged image.

Tapping the Edit button opens a toolbar on the bottom as shown in Figure 11.4.

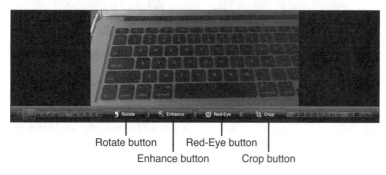

Rotate button   Red-Eye button
       Enhance button   Crop button

FIGURE 11.4   The Edit button enables you to tweak your images.

Tap the Rotate button to rotate the on-screen image counter-clockwise 90 degrees. Each tap rotates the image another 90 degrees.

When you tap the Enhance button the Photos app attempts to provide some color improvements and sharpening of images. When you make edits to a photo you can tap the Save button (see Figure 11.4) to save the image with the enhancements applied, or you can tap the Revert to Original button to cancel any changes you made to the original image.

If you have an image of an individual (or group of people) with red-eye,
tap the Red-Eye button and you are instructed to tap once on each red eye.
The Photos app attempts to fix the image.

Finally, use the Crop button to trim an image and straighten an image that
might have been taken with the camera tilting a bit. The image shown in
Figure 11.5 is the full-sized, original image before using the Crop feature.

FIGURE 11.5   An uncropped photo ready for editing.

After you tap the Crop button, a grid is imposed on top of the original
image. You can drag the top, bottom, left, or right edges as shown in
Figure 11.6 to specify the area of the image you want to retain. In Figure
11.6, the bottom portion of the image has been cropped out.

When you release your finger, the grid centers itself with the image area
you want to save surrounded by the grid. You can then tap the Crop button
in the upper-right corner to apply the crop to the original image or tap the

Reset button at the bottom to try again. Click the Cancel button to completely exit the Crop feature.

Crop button

FIGURE 11.6   Dragging the grid to specify the area of the image to save.

Figure 11.7 shows the newly cropped photo—it's not as tall as the original
but the width is the same.

After you finish editing the image (using the Edit button), you can click
the Cancel button to return to your library of images.

TIP: **Multi-gestures Are Great When Using Photos**

When navigating in and around the Photos app, you might find that
the three-finger pinch multi-gesture comes in handy. When viewing
an image full screen (versus thumbnail), place three fingers on the
screen and pinch them together. This closes the open photo and
returns you to the thumbnail view. A four- or five-finger pinch completely closes the Photos app and returns you to the Home screen.

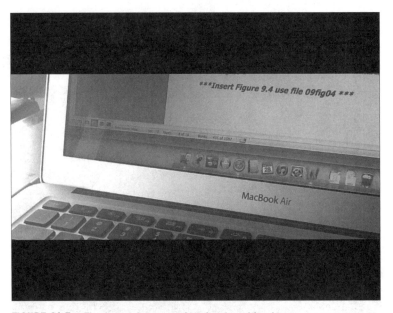

FIGURE 11.7   The image is cropped and reduced in size.

You can likewise tap a video to open and view it. Refer to Lesson 9 for steps on how to trim a video.

Now let's take a look at the other options available in the Photos app. These options include grouping your photos into albums and using the Location Services feature that shows you on a map where a particular photo was taken as well as how to push out your images to other iOS devices using the Photo Stream tool.

Albums

In a nutshell, Albums are the equivalent of folders. You use them to help you better organize your photos. When you take a photo with the Camera app, that photo automatically stores in the Camera Roll album. That's the name of the album, and it cannot be changed. But you can create your own albums (as well as name them) and easily copy photos from the Camera Roll album to your new albums.

There are two methods for creating albums. Let's start with the easier method. Open the Photos app and tap the Photos button called out in Figure 11.2.

Instead of tapping on a photo to enlarge it this time, tap the Action button (see Figure 11.8).

FIGURE 11.8   Using the Move button to organize your photos.

When you tap the Action button, the screen changes slightly as shown in Figure 11.9. Tap those images you want to move to a new album (or click

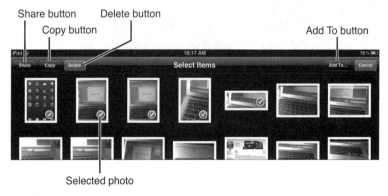

FIGURE 11.9   Selecting images you want to move to a new album.

Cancel to stop the operation). A check appears on the images you tap to indicate they are selected. You can tap the Delete or Copy buttons to delete all checked images or copy them (and thus create identical images in the Camera Roll album).

If you tap the Share button, you are given three options: Email, Print, or Message. Email and Print are self-explanatory. The Message option sends the selected images to a given contact via the Messages app (which is covered in Lesson 6, "Working with Notes, Messages, and Contacts"). If you install Twitter on your iPad, you also see a Tweet option, allowing you to tweet a message with the selected image included.

To move the selected images to a new album, tap the Add To button.

If you've never created any albums of your own, an Add to New Album button displays (see Figure 11.10). If you have existing albums, a button asks you if you want to move the selected photos to an existing album and then enables you to choose an album (other than Camera Roll).

Add to New Album button

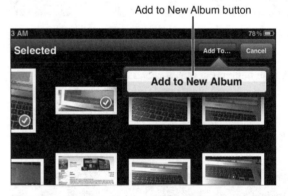

FIGURE 11.10   Creating a new album for your selected images.

In the example shown, there are currently no extra albums created, so if you're following along, tap the Add to New Album button.

Use the on-screen keyboard to name the new album. Tap the Save button when you finish and your new album is created. The selected images auto-matically copy into it as shown in Figure 11.11.

New album   Edit button

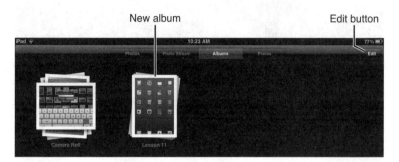

FIGURE 11.11   A new album is created.

Tap the new album to expand it and show all the images inside. Figure 11.12 shows that copies of the five selected images are indeed now included in the new album.

Albums button

FIGURE 11.12   Expanding an album to view thumbnails of its images.

Tap the Albums button to return to the Album view. Now let's see the other method for creating albums.

Tap the Edit button indicated in Figure 11.11. A New Album button dis-plays and an X appears in the upper-left corner of any albums you have previously created (see Figure 11.13).

Tap to delete album
New Album button   Done button

FIGURE 11.13   Creating a new album or deleting an existing one.

If you click the X on an album that album is deleted (but the images inside are still stored in the Camera Roll album). You see a confirmation window asking you to confirm this action.

The New Album button, when tapped, creates an empty folder that you can name with the on-screen keyboard. Immediately after creating the folder, you are taken to the Photos screen and see all the image thumbnails. The Photos screen shows all images stored in the Camera Roll, so you can select images by tapping them (see Figure 11.14).

After you select the images (and videos) to be copied into the new album, tap the Done button and your new album is created (see Figure 11.15).

Keep in mind that when you create new albums and select images, those files are copies of the originals. The original images are kept inside the Camera Roll, at least until you choose to delete them. Deleting an album (that you create) deletes the images inside it, but not their duplicates stored in the Camera Roll.

Photo Stream

If you have multiple iOS devices (such as another iPad or an iPhone or an iPod touch), you can turn on a feature called Photo Stream that uses iCloud (covered in Lesson 13) to automatically place copies of your images that you take with the iPad's Camera app on those other devices.

Tap to move selected photos

FIGURE 11.14   Moving images to a new album.

New album added

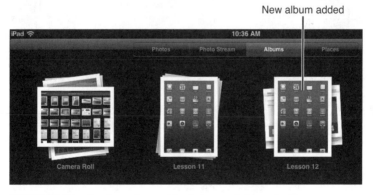

FIGURE 11.15   Another album with photos and videos inside.

This also works in reverse—if you have an iPhone, for example, and have
enabled Photo Stream on both the iPhone and your iPad, any photos you

take with your iPhone are copied (via iCloud) to your iPad and stored in the Photos app.

The only thing you must do is enable the Photo Stream feature. To do this, open the Settings app and tap on the Photos option in the left-side column as shown in Figure 11.16.

Photo Stream feature turned ON

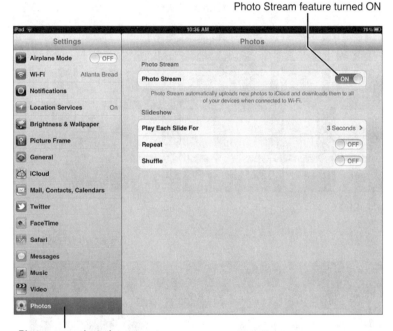

Photos app selected

FIGURE 11.16   Turning on Photo Stream to allow photos to be copied between iOS devices.

Tap the Photo Stream button to turn the feature On or Off. Any iOS device where iCloud is using your Apple ID (and password) begins to share photos if the feature is turned on.

Places

The last feature to discuss in the Photos app is the Places button (see Figure 11.17).

Location of one photo

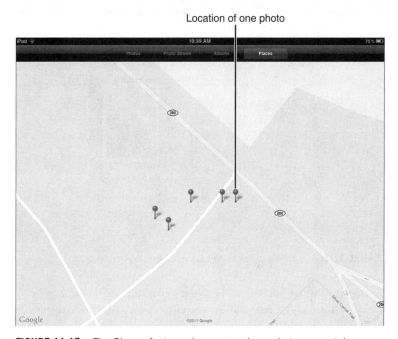

FIGURE 11.17 The Places feature shows you where photos were taken.

In Figure 11.17, there is a map with five red pins on it. If you tap a pin, a thumbnail of a photo taken at that spot displays.

Figure 11.18 shows that a photo of a MacBook Air was taken from a coffee shop on Atlanta Road.

This feature uses the Location Services option discussed in Lesson 2, "Your iPad's Settings." You turn this feature on or off using the

Settings app, and it works by using any combination of Wi-Fi, 3G, or GPS data that your iPad is capable of providing.

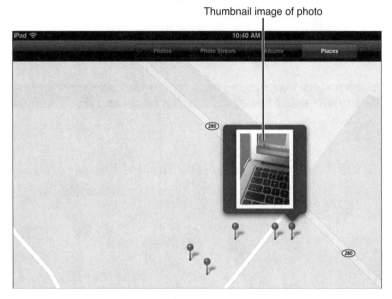

FIGURE 11.18   Viewing a thumbnail taken at a spot on the map.

Examples of where you might like to use this feature are on vacation or maybe while hiking a new trail. As you take photos, Location Services tags each photo with its location, enabling you to go back later and view on a map where each photo was taken. Again, this depends on Location Services being enabled.

There have been some security issues raised with this feature, especially when a person uploads a digital photo to the internet for the entire world to view. A person with the right technical knowledge can obtain the location data stored in a photo and discover where it was taken.

Think carefully about posting photos of your home, your possessions, and even family members on the internet with the location data included. It's a good idea to turn off the ability for the Camera app to add this information.

To disengage this feature, open the Settings app, tap the Location Services option (see Figure 11.19), and then tap the toggle button for the Camera app so it's in the Off position.

Location Services option selected   Camera option turned off

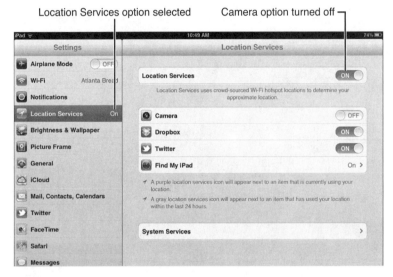

FIGURE 11.19   Turning off the Camera app's ability to embed location data.

Summary

In this lesson you learned how to view photos and videos, how to perform some basic edits using the Photos app, how to organize your images using albums, and how to view where a photo was taken.

Working with Video and YouTube

In this lesson, you learn about the YouTube app and the Videos app. Both are used to watch movies and other video entertainment, but each has its own specialty.

The YouTube App

YouTube is the internet's largest source of both professional and amateur video. From funny animal home videos to feature-length movies filmed with an actual budget and actors, the site enables anyone to upload their videos for the world to watch.

> TIP: **Uploading and Using YouTube Features**
>
> This lesson doesn't offer advice on creating your own videos, uploading them to YouTube, and generating buzz and interest in your creations. This lesson is about using the YouTube app to access the videos available on the YouTube.com website. If you want more information on using YouTube to upload your own videos, *Sams Teach Yourself YouTube in 10 Minutes* is a good resource.

Your iPad comes with an app that gives you access to all the public content available on YouTube. There are videos that are uploaded to YouTube that are not available to just everyone; YouTube allows users to upload video and specify whether it can be viewed by anyone or by a limited audience. The YouTube app on your iPad is only for viewing videos available to everyone, so if a friend tells you about a private video he's uploaded for you and a small number of friends, you need to use a web

browser such as the Safari app and visit YouTube.com. Login with your
YouTube account to prove your identity and access the private content.

Figure 12.1 shows the YouTube app's icon on the iPad. Go ahead and tap it
to open the app.

FIGURE 12.1   The YouTube app icon on your iPad.

When you first open YouTube, you likely see a random assortment of
videos as shown in Figure 12.2. Some of these videos might very well be
offensive to you, so be forewarned; YouTube has very few rules about
what can be shared, and what limitations do exist are primarily related to
pornography and copyrighted content, such as television shows and the-
atrical released movies. Everything else is pretty much fair game.

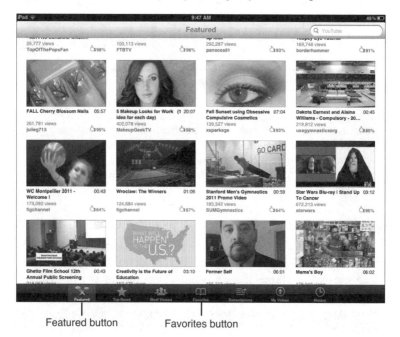

Featured button   Favorites button

FIGURE 12.2   YouTube presents you with a random assortment of videos.

After the first time you open YouTube, it always returns to the screen you last viewed. The first time you open the YouTube app, however, it starts on the Featured page, a mix of newly uploaded videos that YouTube chooses to present to the general public.

If you don't like the video thumbnails you see when you first open YouTube, don't worry. You can find what you want to watch and change the thumbnails to subject matter that is more relevant to your tastes.

In Figure 12.2 notice a toolbar with seven different buttons along the bottom of the screen. Right now, the screen displays the Featured videos, but go ahead and tap the Favorites button to clear the screen temporarily. If this is your first time opening the YouTube app, this screen should be empty of videos as shown in Figure 12.3.

Begin by using the Search bar in the upper-right corner of the screen to search for a topic that interests you. Figure 12.4 shows a search for funny cat videos and the resulting thumbnails show me that the search was fruitful.

FIGURE 12.3   The Favorites screen is empty at first.

To play a video, simply tap a thumbnail and the video opens in full screen as shown in Figure 12.5.

Search keywords

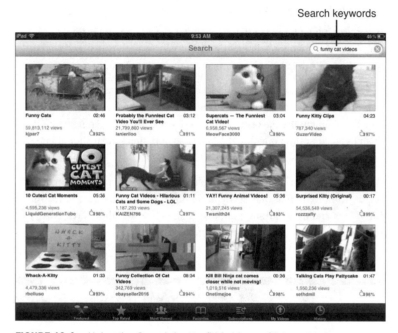

FIGURE 12.4   Using the Search bar to find videos of interest to you.

Tap the screen with one finger to view the controls, such as Pause and Play. If you tap the Done button anytime during the video, the current video shrinks and displays on the left along with other search results on the right as shown in Figure 12.6. (You can also use a two-finger pinch to perform the same action as the Done button.)

Notice in Figure 12.6 that this screen offers a large number of options. Tap the Add button to add the video to your Favorites category. Tap the Share button to email a link to the video to a contact or attach it to a tweet (via the Twitter app). Tap the Comments button to view comments left by other viewers (often crude and insulting, so be careful), or tap a new video on the right side of the screen to watch a different search result find.

Done button   Video progress bar

On screen controls

FIGURE 12.5   A selected YouTube video playing full screen.

Notice also in Figure 12.6 that the toolbar is still visible along the bottom of the screen. The Top Rated and Most Viewed buttons take you to a screen containing a mixture of video topics based on popularity votes and number of views, respectively.

The Favorites button functions like the Bookmark feature in Safari. When you tap the Add button and select Favorites, a thumbnail of that video is stored so you can view again at a later time.

If you find one or more videos from the same source (a person or organization) that you enjoy, you can choose to subscribe to that video source. You must first create a YouTube account and log in to do this. Next, tap the More From button indicated in Figure 12.7 and then tap the Subscribe button.

Share button

Add button

Additional videos
that satisfy search

Top Rated button

Most Viewed button

FIGURE 12.6   Viewing a smaller version of the video next to more search results.

More From   Subsribe button

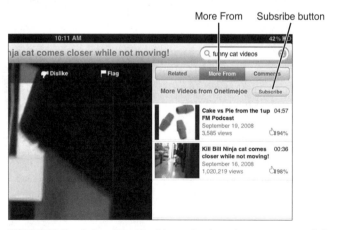

FIGURE 12.7   Subscribing to video uploaders that you want to follow.

After you subscribe, tap the Subscriptions button on the toolbar and then tap the username on the left. This displays all videos from that source on the right side of the screen (see Figure 12.8). This is a nice way to quickly check on new releases without having to remember the username and use the Search bar.

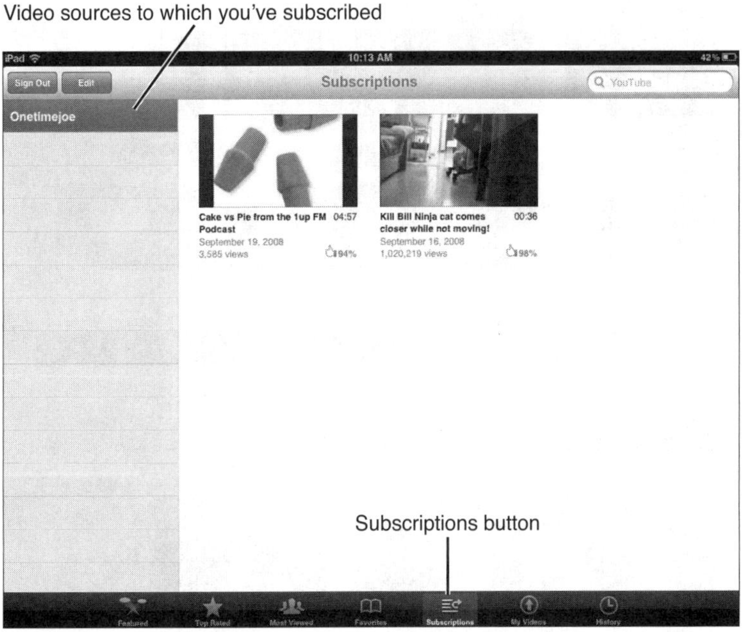

Video sources to which you've subscribed

FIGURE 12.8   Use Subscriptions to stay up-to-date on favorite video uploaders.

If you have previously loaded any videos to YouTube, you can tap the My Videos button to view thumbnails of your own video content (see Figure 12.9). Keep in mind that this also requires that you login to YouTube with a valid user account.

Finally, tap the History button to view thumbnails of your previously viewed videos (see Figure 12.10).

The YouTube app is simple and efficient, but it is limited to public videos that are uploaded to the YouTube service. To watch TV shows or movies, you need to use the Videos app.

My Videos button

FIGURE 12.9   View your own YouTube videos.

History button

FIGURE 12.10   Your video viewing history is always available.

CAUTION: **YouTube Requires a Data Connection**
The YouTube app is all about providing quick and easy access to the YouTube video content, but there is a limitation. The YouTube app requires a Wi-Fi or 3G data connection because YouTube content is not stored on your iPad. There are apps that enable you to download YouTube videos for offline viewing. Search the App Store for "offline YouTube video" to find them.

The Videos App

Your iPad is a great device for web browsing, emailing, listening to music, and even taking pictures. But the full-color screen is also capable of displaying the latest in Hollywood movies and television shows in both widescreen and standard format.

Before you watch a movie, you must open the Videos app on your iPad. To do this, tap the Videos app icon shown in Figure 12.11.

FIGURE 12.11   The Videos app icon on your iPad.

Tap the Videos app icon to launch the app. If you have not previously purchased or rented video content from iTunes, an empty screen greets you, as shown in Figure 12.12.

Apple gives you two methods for browsing and purchasing or renting movies and TV shows. You can tap the Store button or you can tap the tiny arrow indicated in Figure 12.12. Either choice opens iTunes and takes you to the Movies section (see Figure 12.13). (Refer to Lesson 10, "Listening to Music," for more information on iTunes.)

Store button

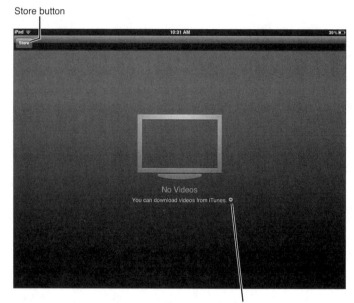

Tap to open iTunes to browse movies

FIGURE 12.12 An empty video library.

New Release suggestions

FIGURE 12.13 The Movies section of iTunes.

As with the iBooks Store or the App Store, the Movies section of iTunes attempts to help you find what you want by offering up suggested new releases near the top of the screen (indicated in Figure 12.13) and categories and rentals near the bottom of the screen as shown in Figure 12.14.

Category buttons

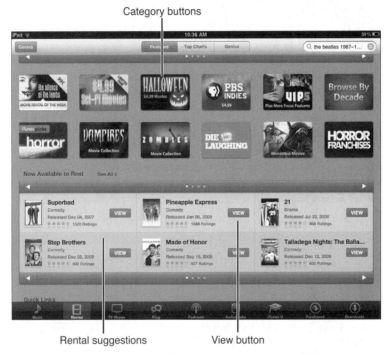

Rental suggestions   View button

FIGURE 12.14   Categories and rentals in the Movies section.

You can also use the Search bar to find a specific movie or TV show title or even search for genres or keywords. Every movie or TV show thumbnail you find has a View button, which you can tap to see an information screen like the one in Figure 12.15.

The information screen displays a summary of the movie or TV show episode (or entire season) as well as reviews (scroll to the bottom). You might see a Preview button that shows you a short preview of the video you're looking at.

Summary details   Preview button

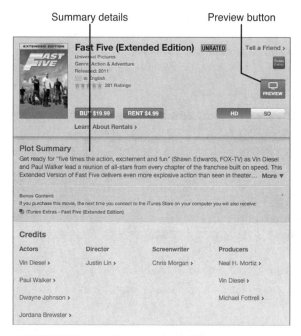

FIGURE 12.15   Opening a movie or TV show's information screen.

Some videos are only for purchase; others are only for rent. If you see both buttons available, tap your choice and the video begins to download to the iPad. Keep in mind that rentals are only available for 24 hours, but you can stop, pause, restart, or even rewatch the video as many times as you like during that 24-hour period. You have 30 days to start watching a rental, but the 24-hour clock starts ticking down the moment you push Play for the first time. When those 24 hours are up, the video disappears from the Videos library.

Purchasing a video, however, puts it on your iPad permanently, or at least until you back it up and remove it from the iPad using iTunes. Use the iTunes Help feature for more information on backing up your music and videos before deleting them to free up space.

Speaking of space, do keep in mind that every movie or TV show you download takes up a good bit of storage space. If you have a 16GB or 32GB iPad, keep an eye on your storage space in the Settings app.

After you purchase or rent a movie, it begins to download to your Library. Tap the Downloads button (see Figure 12.16) to see the progress. (Note that you can tap the Pause button at any time to pause the download.)

NOTE: Downloading Videos Takes Some Time

Downloading a purchased or rented movie to your iPad can take some time, especially with Wi-Fi and 3G data speeds. If you lose your Wi-Fi or 3G connection, the download pauses and starts up again when a signal is reacquired.

When the download completes you can tap the thumbnail shown in Figure 12.16 to open and play the video. Because the video download is likely to take a while, you might want to leave and return to the video a bit later.

Download progress bar

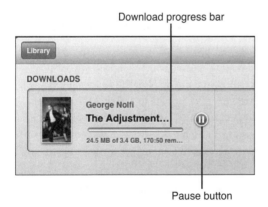

Pause button

FIGURE 12.16   Your video download begins.

Open the Videos app later to find a larger thumbnail of your download as shown in Figure 12.17. Tap the thumbnail to play your movie.

Tap to start movie

FIGURE 12.17   Downloaded movies or TV shows are listed in the Videos app.

Tap the screen to either display or hide the video controls, as shown in Figure 12.18.

As you can see, buying and renting movies and TV shows on your iPad is simple. But what if you already own a movie on DVD and want to view it on your iPad? It's possible to rip a DVD movie to a digital file and then copy that file to your iPad (via iTunes). It's not a difficult process, but it does require a series of steps longer than this lesson allows. Point your web browser to the following web article I wrote if you want to learn how to do this:

http://www.quepublishing.com/articles/article.aspx?p=1655237

If you own the DVD and want to back it up to view it on your iPad, please do so, but don't share your ripped movies with friends—that's illegal.

Movie progress bar

Tap on screen to view controls

FIGURE 12.18 Video controls are visible.

Also, DVDs come with built-in anti-copying technology. The article shows you how to get around that, but some newer DVDs are not able to be ripped with the DVDShrink application mentioned in the article. If you find a movie cannot be ripped with DVDShrink, do a web search for DVDFab, a good substitute for ripping DVD movies.

Summary

In this lesson, you learned all about the YouTube and Videos apps. You learned how to search, find, and watch YouTube videos that interest you as well as search for movies and TV shows that you can buy or rent using iTunes.

Other Interesting Uses for the iPad

With iOS 5, iPad users get access to a variety of new services and features. In this lesson, you are introduced to some of them and shown where to find more details on all the new additions to the latest version of iOS.

Non-App Features

Throughout this book, you've learned how to use the basic apps included with iOS 5. Many of these apps have been around since the release of the first iPad, such as Mail and Safari and App Store; but a few new ones, such as Newsstand and Reminders, continue to make the iPad a more productive tool.

With the new iOS 5, Apple added some behind-the-scenes features that are just waiting for iPad users to discover them. Apple didn't hide them to be tricky. Instead, some of the features are just hidden from view because they work to make your iPad more secure from the moment you turn on your iPad. An example of this is the iCloud service you read about shortly. Some features are turned off, and you simply need to turn them on, such as the built-in support for Twitter. If you have a Twitter account, you can tweet directly from your iPad whenever you like. And if you're not a Twitter user, you never need to worry with this feature.

There are other new services that you learn about shortly, but let's get started by looking at iCloud, a service that you're sure to love as it can help ensure that your music, photos, and more are protected if your iPad becomes damaged, lost, or stolen.

iCloud

iCloud isn't an app that you open. Instead, you access its settings through the Settings app. Tap the Settings app and then select the iCloud option from the Settings List as shown in Figure 13.1.

iCloud option ——

FIGURE 13.1   Accessing iCloud from your Settings menu.

Here's how iCloud works in a nutshell.

First, when you buy your iPad (or other Apple device), you are provided an automatic 5GB (gigabytes) of data storage by Apple. This is storage space that Apple provides to you for free and it serves two purposes.

▸ Backup:With the proper configuration (you learn this technique next), iCloud can back up your photos, your music, your contacts, and much more. If your iPad becomes lost or damaged (or retired), you can retrieve all those items that are backed up with iCloud and put them either right back on your repaired iPad or on your newly purchased iPad.

▶ Synchronization: You can configure devices such as an iPhone or iPod touch or Apple computer (or even a PC) to use iCloud to keep your photos, contacts, email, and more synchronized across all your devices. Using Wi-Fi or 3G, iCloud ensures that no matter which device you are currently using, you have instant access to your pictures, music, and more.

NOTE: **5GB Is More Than You Think**

When tracking the 5 gigabytes of storage space that iCloud offers to you, keep in mind that your purchased music (from iTunes), books, movies, and apps do not count against you. If you purchase 1GB of music from iTunes, that 1GB of backed-up music via iCloud is in addition to the 5GB you receive when you create your Apple ID and sign up for iCloud. But if you find you need more storage space from iCloud, Apple offers a number of reasonably priced upgrades.

Because iCloud works behind the scenes, after you set it in motion you might never need to deal with its settings again. So, after selecting the iCloud option in the Settings app, you should see a list of items running down the right side of the screen as shown in Figure 13.2. This list includes Mail, Contacts, Calendars, Reminders, Bookmarks, Notes, Photos, Documents & Data, and something called Find My iPad.

If you leave a toggle button set to the On position (such as for Contacts, shown in Figure 13.2), then this means that you want iCloud to back up the information in the Contacts app. You can backup phone numbers, addresses, birthdays...literally everything.

As you can see in Figure 13.2, iCloud is backing up calendar appointments, web bookmarks, and even reminders. But take a closer look and you see that neither Mail nor Notes are included in the backup (the toggle switch for each is set to Off). If you use Gmail (Google Mail), your email is stored (and backed up) by Google. You could still choose to use iCloud to back up your Google mail, but if you have a lot of messages and a lot of attachments, it would easily run over the free 5GB.

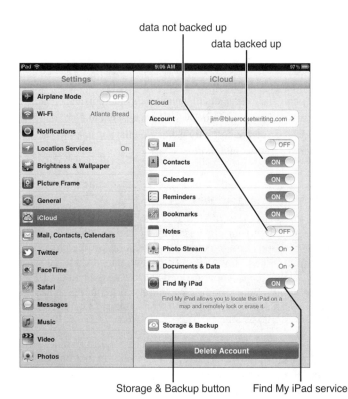

FIGURE 13.2 Choosing what data you want to backup to iCloud.

Find My iPad is a new service from Apple that allows your iPad to send its current location (if Location Services in the Settings app is turned to On). If your iPad becomes lost or stolen, the next time it connects to the internet it sends its location to iCloud, enabling you to use the Find My iPad service to locate the iPad. There's no obvious reason to disable this feature, but you can easily tap the toggle button to turn it off.

Tap the Storage & Backup button to see a screen like the one featured in Figure 13.3.

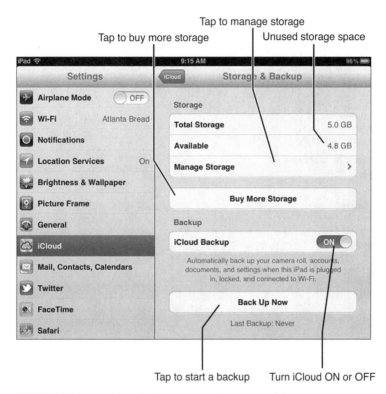

FIGURE 13.3   Your iCloud information and upgrade options.

To turn off the iCloud backup service, tap the iCloud Backup toggle button indicated in Figure 13.3. Confirm this action on the pop-up window that appears. You can also choose to back up to iCloud as long as you have a wireless connection (Wi-Fi or 3G). To do this, tap the Back Up Now button. Keep in mind that this can take a while if you have a lot of data to backup.

On this screen you also find information related to how much storage you have available. If you find that you need more space, simply click the Buy More Storage button and a window like the one shown in Figure 13.4 displays.

Tap a storage space option   Tap to buy more space

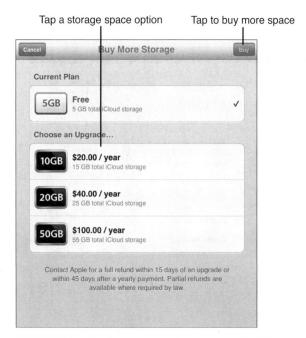

FIGURE 13.4   Purchasing more storage space for iCloud.

You can purchase more storage space, increasing the 5GB by 10GB, 20GB, or even 50GB (for total storage space of 15GB, 25GB, and 55GB respectively). Tap an upgrade to select it and then click the Buy button.

Finally, keep in mind that even though the apps you purchase are not counted against your 5GB of space, any data they create and store, consumes storage space. You can control whether iCloud backs up app data by turning On or Off the Documents & Data button. This is an all-or-nothing selection, so if you want to select data on an app-by-app basis, you must tap the Manage Storage button indicated in Figure 13.3. This opens a window like the one shown in Figure 13.5.

The total amount of data that is currently being backed up is shown in Figure 13.5, but this can be edited. Tap anywhere in the top button (with the iPad icon) and a new screen like the one in Figure 13.6 opens, enabling you to choose the data you want to back up.

Tap button to view more details

Total size of data being backed up

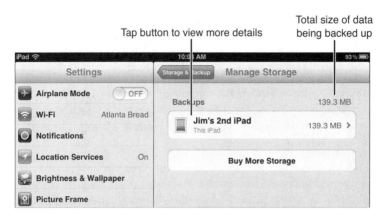

FIGURE 13.5   Managing the storage of your apps and data.

App data will be backed up

App data will not be backed up

Tap to delete iCloud backup

FIGURE 13.6   Turning off apps to disable a backup of their data.

On this screen you can choose one or more apps and set their toggle buttons to Off to disable iCloud's ability to back up their respective data. In the example shown, the data created by the AnotherWorld app doesn't need to be saved, so the toggle is set to the Off position.

Finally, tap the big red Delete Backup button to delete the current iCloud backup completely. You might choose to do this to purge your iCloud account and start over with a more controlled backup where you turn off some apps and their data backup.

The iCloud service is a good insurance against damage or loss of your iPad. Keep an eye on the total storage space used and upgrade if you have to, but sleep soundly knowing your apps, music, photos, emails, and much more can all be recovered in a worst-case scenario.

Twitter

Twitter is everywhere. If you're not familiar with it, you can find a wealth of information on how it works and what people use it for by visiting http://www.twitter.com.

If you're a current Twitter user, you'll be happy to know that iOS 5 has built-in Twitter support that enables you to send tweets while working in many of the basic apps such as Camera, Safari, Photos, and a few others.

The Twitter app is not installed on your iPad when you purchase it. To install the app, open the Settings app, select the Twitter item in the Settings List, and then tap the Install button shown in Figure 13.7.

The installation happens outside of the App Store. The app automatically installs on your Home screen (see Figure 13.8).

Return to the Settings app and the Twitter configuration screen shown in Figure 13.7 and log in with your Twitter username and password. Your iPad stores this information and keeps you logged in continually as you use other apps on your iPad.

After you log in, you can use the Twitter app installed on your iPad to send a tweet. When the app opens, tap on the New Tweet button indicated in Figure 13.9.

Click to install Twitter app

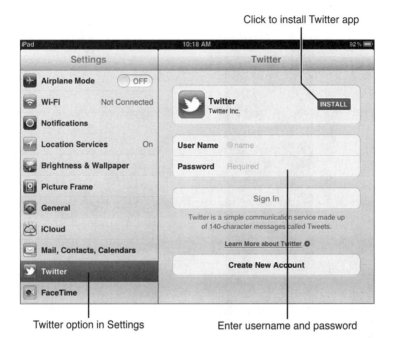

Twitter option in Settings   Enter username and password

FIGURE 13.7   Installing Twitter on your iPad.

FIGURE 13.8   The Twitter app installed on your iPad.

Type your tweet (140 characters or shorter) and tap the Send button (see Figure 13.10). Twitter tools, such as the # and @, are available and you can also use buttons to attach a photo or specify the location of the tweet.

Even when you don't run the Twitter app, certain apps enable you to quickly send a tweet. For example, you can open a photo with the Photos app (see Lesson 11, "Using the Photos App") and tap the Send button—along with the Email and Print options there's a Tweet option.

Tap to create new tweet

FIGURE 13.9   Using the Twitter app to send a tweet.

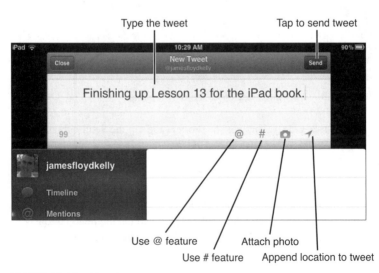

Type the tweet

Tap to send tweet

Use @ feature

Use # feature

Attach photo

Append location to tweet

FIGURE 13.10   Tweeting a message.

Tap the Tweet button to open a message window like the one in Figure 13.11. This enables you to type a fast tweet (and include the location if you want) and send it on its way.

FIGURE 13.11   Typing and sending a tweet without leaving the Photos app.

Not all apps offer this ability, so you have to search for apps that support this feature. Figure 13.12, for example, shows the Safari app open and running. If you find a web page you want to tweet about, tap the Send button to find the Tweet option.

Tweet option in Safari

FIGURE 13.12   Tweeting from within the Safari app.

Computer-Free Activation and Auto-Updates via Wi-Fi

When the iPad was first released, it required a Mac or PC computer to activate the tablet. You had to connect the iPad to a computer via USB and sync it with iTunes. That's no longer the case.

Now, when you turn on an iPad with iOS 5 installed, you can set up the iPad via a Wi-Fi network. No computer is required.

Another added benefit of the iPad's independent operation is the ability for iOS 5 to update itself without connecting to a computer. As Apple releases updates to the operating system, you find a small badge similar to the one that appears on the App Store or Mail app to alert you to updates and new messages. This alert lets you know that Apple has released an update, and all you must do to install it is open the Settings app and tap the Software Update option (see Figure 13.13).

Tap to check for updates

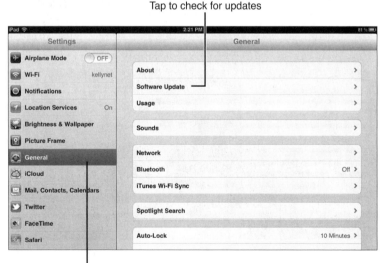

General option in Settings app

FIGURE 13.13   Applying updates to your iPad as they are released.

Follow the instructions to have the update applied automatically.

This feature enables you to quickly apply fixes and updates to your iPad without the need to connect to a computer via USB to download an update.

Put the iPad on the Big Screen

If you have an HDTV connected to an Apple TV device, you'll find that your iPad 2 running iOS 5 can now send whatever you see on the iPad's touchscreen directly to the HDTV screen using AirPlay.

The Apple TV device (see Figure 13.14) enables you to download shows and movies over the internet, but this ability to control the TV with your iPad is a nice feature for Apple TV owners to try.

Apple TV Device

FIGURE 13.14   Pair your iPad with the Apple TV to send images to a bigger screen.

The Newsstand App

With the release of iOS 5, a new app has been added that works similarly to the iBook app. It's called Newsstand and it's basically a shelf that holds magazines and newspapers for which you have a subscription. What's nice about the Newsstand app is that once you purchase a subscription to a newspaper or magazine, the app automatically updates the shelf with the latest edition of your subscriptions.

In the case of a daily newspaper, you simply tap the Newsstand app each day to read the day's news. With magazines, you find the latest issue on your shelf on the day the issue is released for sale in bookstores.

Figure 13.15 shows the Newsstand App. Tap the Store button or the white card in the center of the shelf to open the Newsstand section of iTunes to purchase magazine or newspaper subscriptions. You can also purchase individual issues of magazines (if the magazine offers that ability) if you don't want an on-going subscription.

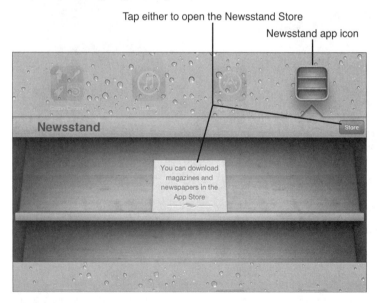

FIGURE 13.15   Visit the Newsstand app to buy and read magazines and newspapers.

Navigate the Newsstand store much like you would navigate the iBook store, locating and finding a magazine or newspaper you wish to read on your iPad. As shown in Figure 13.16, you see a variety of magazines and newspapers with a Free button which can be a bit confusing at first.

Tap to install Free Subscriber Tool

FIGURE 13.16 The Free button only installs the free subscribe tool.

After you tap an icon (typically with a Free button), it installs what can be called a free subscriber tool on the bookshelf, not the actual magazine or newspaper. To get the digital periodical, you must complete one more step.

After you install the free subscriber tool for a magazine or newspaper, it appears on the shelf as shown in Figure 13.17. Tap the image representing the magazine or book to view purchase options.

Figure 13.18 shows the option to purchase single issues of *Wired* magazine or to subscribe.

Tap to open Free Subscriber Tool

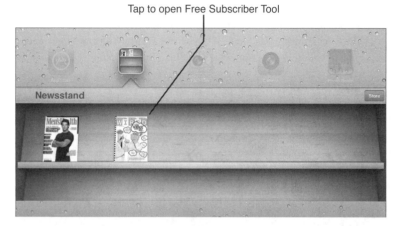

FIGURE 13.17 Tap on an image to buy or subscribe.

Tap to Subscribe

Tap to purchase current issue

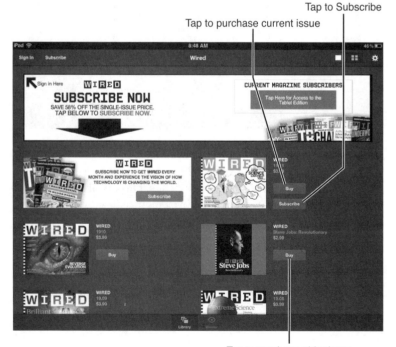

Tap to purchase older issue

FIGURE 13.18 Current and past issues can be purchased.

As you can see in Figure 13.18, not only is a subscription available along with the option to purchase only the current issue, but you also have the option to purchase previous issues of the magazine. This feature isn't available with all magazine and newspaper subscriptions, however.

The Newsstand app is a nice way to keep your iPad's home screens from becoming cluttered with numerous magazine and newspaper app icons. Before iOS 5, if you had four or five magazine subscriptions, each magazine would place an app icon on a home screen. This may not seem like a big deal, but if you didn't keep all your subscription apps on the same home screen, it meant a lot of swiping to find what you wanted to read. Not anymore. Now the Newsstand app is your one-stop-shop for browsing, buying, and reading all your subscriptions.

The Photo Booth App

One final new app that you find with iOS 5 is the Photo Booth app. This fun little app uses the iPad's built-in webcam or digital camera. As you can see in Figure 13.19, a total of nine different special effects are applied to what the webcam initially sees. (Actually, it's eight because the center special effect is simply called Normal.)

Tap on a special effect (such as X-Ray) and decide if you want to use either the webcam or the digital camera by tapping the Toggle View button. When you like what you see, tap the Shutter button and your image is stored in the Photos app Camera Roll album. Finally, tap the Effects button to return to the nine special effects option (shown in Figure 13.18).

The Photo Booth app isn't a professional level photo editing tool—instead, it simply provides you with some fun effects that can be applied to your photos. Currently, these effects can only be applied to new images taken with the Photo Booth app, not to your previously existing images in the Photos app, but this could change with an app update later.

Normal Effect   X-Ray Effect

FIGURE 13.19 The Photo App applies special effects to the webcam.

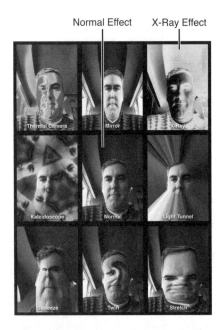

New Operating System, New Features

With the release of iOS 5, Apple released a number of new apps and new features for the iPad user. You have the Messages, Reminders, and Newsstand apps combined with the iCloud service and integrated Twitter functionality. The Notifications bar that hides at the top of the screen is a great way to stay organized and informed without filling your screen with dozens of reminders, new message alerts, and update notifications.

As Apple continues to improve the operating system, expect to be using the Software Update feature mentioned earlier in this lesson to keep your iPad installed with the latest and greatest fixes, improvements, and new apps.

Summary

In this lesson you learned about some of the new features added to the iOS operating system with version 5. You learned how to use iCloud, how to use the built-in Twitter tool, and other new services that make using your iPad easier and more efficient.

Index

E

Edit button, Photos app, 185
editing features, Camera, 158-159
email
  archiving, 80
  forwarding messages, 75
  Gmail accounts, configuring,
    69-71
  messages, checking for, 71-74
  organizing, 78-82
  replying to, 74-76
  sending, 77-78
Enhance button, Photos app, 185
exterior of iPad, 7

F

FaceTime, 161-165
face-to-face chats, FaceTime,
  161-165
Favorites button, YouTube app, 201
Featured button, App Store, 124
Find My iPad, 218
folders, 28
  creating for apps (App Store),
    136-137
forwarding messages, email, 75
four-finger pinch, 24
four-finger slide, 24
four-finger swipe, 25-26

G

General item, 44-46
Genius button, App Store, 124
gestures, 18
  dragging, 19
  four-finger pinch, 24
  four-finger slide, 24
  four-finger swipe, 25-26
  pinching, 19-22
  reverse pinching, 22-24
  swiping, 19
Gmail, 68
Gmail accounts, configuring, 69-71
GoodReader app, 47
Grid option, Camera, 157

H

headphones, 12
History, 60
History button, YouTube app, 205
Home button, 14
Home screen, 15-16
  additional screens, 26-28
Horizontal View, Notes, 104
hyperlinks, copying, 56-57

W

Y

Z

Sams**TeachYourself**

from Sams Publishing

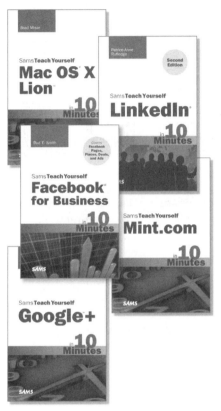

Sams Teach Yourself in 10 Minutes
offers straightforward, practical answers
for fast results.

These small books of 250 pages or less
offer tips that point out shortcuts and
solutions, cautions that help you avoid
common pitfalls, and notes that explain
additional concepts and provide additional
information. By working through the
10-minute lessons, you learn everything
you need to know quickly and easily!

When you only have time for the answers,
Sams Teach Yourself books are your
best solution.

Visit **informit.com/samsteachyourself**
for a complete listing of the products
available.

FREE Online Edition

Your purchase of **Sams Teach Yourself iPad 2 in 10 Minutes** includes access to a free online edition for 45 days through the Safari Books Online subscription service. Nearly every Sams book is available online through Safari Books Online, along with more than 5,000 other technical books and videos from publishers such as Addison-Wesley Professional, Cisco Press, Exam Cram, IBM Press, O'Reilly, Prentice Hall, and Que.

SAFARI BOOKS ONLINE allows you to search for a specific answer, cut and paste code, download chapters, and stay current with emerging technologies.

Activate your FREE Online Edition at www.informit.com/safarifree

STEP 1: Enter the coupon code: PZKGHFH.

STEP 2: New Safari users, complete the brief registration form. Safari subscribers, just log in.

If you have difficulty registering on Safari or accessing the online edition, please e-mail customer-service@safaribooksonline.com